W9-CFB-903

Thailand

Thailand

BY SYLVIA MCNAIR

Enchantment of the World
Second Series

Children's Press®

A Division of Grolier Publishing

NEW YORK   LONDON   HONG KONG   SYDNEY
DANBURY, CONNECTICUT

Thailand

23037

For Toon, with affection and gratitude.

Consultant: Larry Ashmun, The Asia Society, New York City

Please note: All figures are as up-to-date as possible at the time of publication.

Visit Children's Press on the Internet: http://publishing.grolier.com

Book production by Editorial Directions, Inc.
Book design by Ox+Company, Inc.

Library of Congress Cataloging-in-Publication Data

McNair, Sylvia.
      Thailand / Sylvia McNair.
      p. cm. — (Enchantment of the world. Second series)
Summary: Explores the geography, history, arts, religion, and everyday life of Thailand.
      ISBN 0-516-21100-5
      1. Thailand—Juvenile literature. [1. Thailand.] I. Title. II. Series
      DS563.5.M36 1998
      959.3—dc21   CIP
                                                      AC

Acknowledgments

The author is grateful to the Tourist Authority of Thailand for its generosity over the years in supplying information and help. Special thanks go to Carmelita Marsh, of the TAT Chicago office. Thai Air and the Royal Thai Embassy have also been helpful. Thanks to Joe Cummings, a colleague and long-time resident of Thailand, for writing such good guidebooks to Thailand. Thanks also to Allen McNair and Anna Idol, who read the final manuscript and made useful suggestions.

Finally, thanks to a longtime friend, Varakorn Mangclasiri, who has gone out of his way to help keep alive the author's interest in the Land of Smiles.

Contents

Cover photo:
Young Buddhist monks

A fishing village
in Panyi

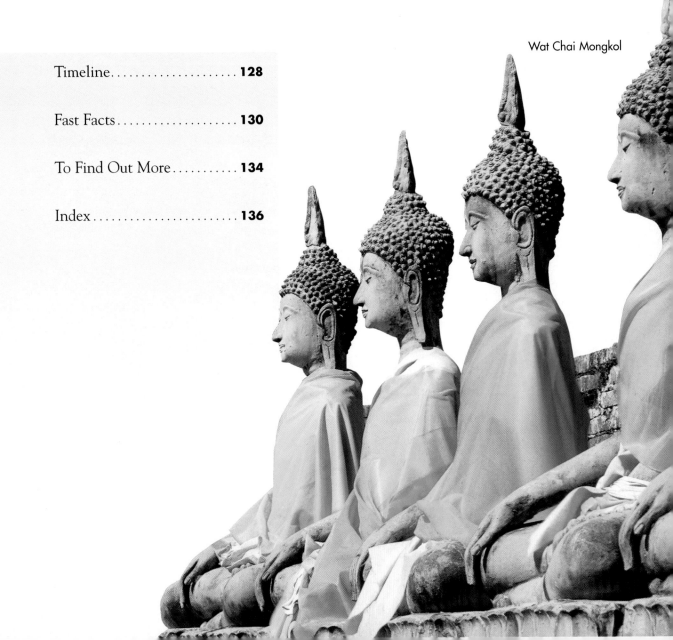

Wat Chai Mongkol

Welcome to the Land of Smiles

What is Thailand, this ancient place once called Siam? It is a land of golden spires, gleaming temples, and modern cities. It is jungles, sandy beaches, and mountain ranges that fade away on a distant misty horizon. It is water buffalo trudging beside bright-green rice paddies, elephants lumbering down steep forested trails, and monkeys chattering as they leap from tree to tree.

I T IS A LAND OF SMILES, A PLACE OF gentle people who greet friends and strangers alike with a polite bow. In Thailand, more than 60 million people are united by a common language, a greatly beloved and respected king, and a shared belief in Buddhism.

To get acquainted with Thai people, one should learn a few Thai customs. The first one is *wai*—the polite bow Thais use when meeting others. To make a wai, press both your hands together with the fingers pointing upward, thumbs inward, and arms close at the sides. At the same time, bow your head toward your thumbs.

A Buddhist novice at ordination

Thais do not really expect a *farang* (foreigner) to make a wai. Certain rules dictate how deeply one should bow, according to the relative status of the two people involved. Foreigners who do not know these rules may prefer to shake hands. Most Thais realize that a handshake is customary in other countries and are comfortable using it to greet or say good-bye to farangs.

Opposite: **The Grand Palace in Bangkok**

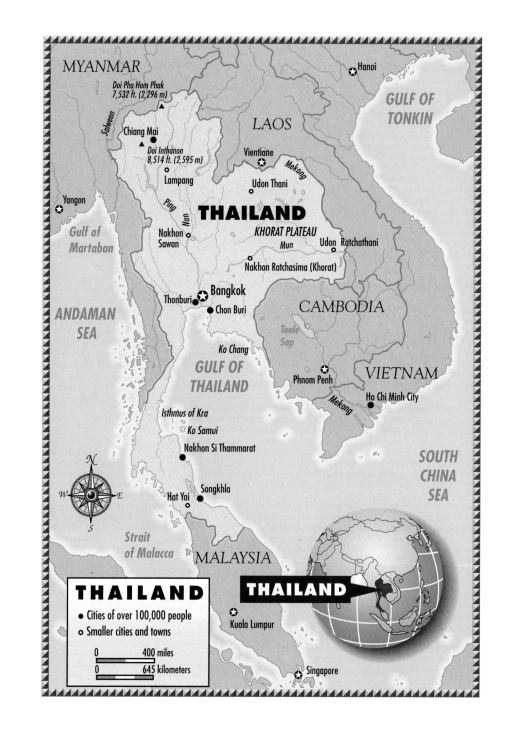

Geopolitical map of Thailand

Another word that tells a lot about the Thai way of life is *sanuk*. In English, the closest translation is "fun," but sanuk means more than that. To be sanuk means to enjoy whatever one is doing, to take things lightly, and to keep a sense of humor. Sanuk is not only for leisure activities—working should be sanuk, too. Then there is *mai pen rai*, a favorite expression in Thailand. It means "it doesn't matter," "don't worry about it," or "no problem," as well as "you're welcome."

Thais are generally very patient and tolerant. They smile no matter what is happening. That doesn't necessarily mean, however, that they agree with or approve of another person's point of view. They say "mai pen rai" when problems occur. They try to find sanuk in every situation.

As one Thai businessperson explains it, "We're tolerant even when people are doing the wrong thing. In a traffic jam, we don't sound our horns; we take out our cell phones and get some work done."

What Is Thailand Really Like?

A farang on a first visit to Thailand will probably start with Bangkok. Bangkok is big, crowded, noisy, polluted—but also lively and exciting. It has wonderful temples, monuments, and museums, as well as peaceful parks and gardens. Its leading hotels are among the best in the world. Bangkok is the nation's cultural and business hub, as well as its center of government.

To know Thailand, a visitor must explore the countryside. Thailand is mostly a nation of villages. Four of every five

Thais live in a rural area. Each village has a Buddhist monastery called a *wat*. A wat has several buildings, used for religious meditation and for many other community activities. Buddhism was introduced to Thailand many centuries ago, and about 95 percent of the people are Buddhists. From the mountains of the north to the beaches of the south and from the bustling cities to the quiet villages, getting acquainted with Thailand's scenery, its long history, and, above all, its people, is definitely sanuk!

Bangkok, along the Chao Phraya River at sunset

CHAPTER TWO

A Bountiful Nature

"The forests abound with vegetables and exquisite fruits. The rivers, the lakes, the ponds teem with fish. . . . the lands [are] wonderfully fertile. Man has but to sow and plant."

THAT'S HOW A FRENCH EXPLORER DESCRIBED THE NATURAL richness of Thailand—then called Siam—when he traveled across the country in 1858. He marveled at the abundance of wildlife—monkeys, crocodiles, and birds. He called the Siamese a lucky people, "spoiled by a bountiful nature."

Some people say that a map of Thailand looks like the head of an elephant, with its long trunk hanging down. Others describe its shape as an ax, its handle hanging down toward the south. Still other people suggest it is like a flower with a ragged stem. The neighboring countries of Myanmar (formerly known as Burma), Laos, and Cambodia wrap around the head of the flower. The stem stretches down a long peninsula between the Andaman Sea and the Gulf of Thailand, ending at the border of Malaysia. Its total area is about the size of France.

Thailand has four major land types. Lofty mountains tower above the far north and along the western border with Myanmar. The highest peak is Doi Inthanon, at 8,514 feet (2,595 m). Forests of evergreen and teak trees cover the lower slopes. Elephants were used here to transport lumber to

A view of the Golden Triangle, which includes parts of Myanmar and Laos

market, before recent restrictions on tree-cutting. Mountain streams flow down to join larger rivers.

The northeast is a rolling landscape, part of the Khorat Plateau. This plateau stretches eastward into Laos and Cambodia. The soil in the northeast is thin and gets less rainfall than in other regions. Occasional droughts and floods make farming more difficult than in the central plains. The Mekong River is the main boundary with Laos in the north and northeast.

The central plains are very fertile, making this one of the best rice-growing areas in the world. The Chao Phraya River courses through its wide, fairly flat valley.

The southern peninsula is a long, narrow strip of land. It is primarily a rain forest, mountainous and dense with trees and shrubs. The coastal plains are lined with gorgeous beaches, and there are hundreds of offshore islands. Waterfalls, hot springs, and caves are among the area's natural attractions. Colorful fish and coral formations bring scuba divers to this part of the country.

Coral reefs along the coast attract snorkelers and scuba divers.

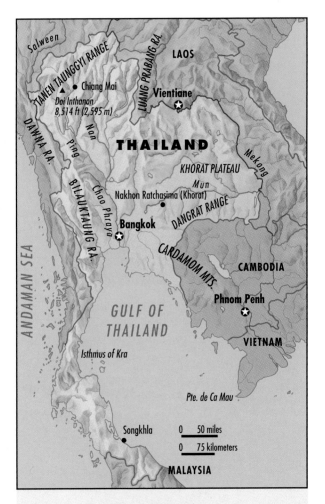

Geographical Features

Area: 198,115 sq. mi. (513,115 sq km)

Highest Elevation: Doi Inthanon, 8,514 feet (2,595 m)

Lowest Elevation: Sea level

Longest River: Chao Phraya River, 225 miles (365 km)

Largest City: Bangkok

Average Annual Precipitation: In the north, west, and
central regions, 60 inches (152 cm)
On the Khorat Plateau, 50 inches (127 cm)

Thailand has a tropical climate, with three seasons. Official sources call them cool, hot, and rainy, but some people say there are only two kinds of weather in Thailand—hot and not-so-hot!

The so-called cool season is from November to February. From March to April is the hot season, and the rainy season is from May to October. In the south, however, there are really only two seasons. Rainfall is heavy in this part of the country for most of the year. The only dry months are March and April.

Most of Thailand, except the mountains and the Khorat Plateau, is very humid. Temperatures range from a low of 46°F (8°C) at night in the north during the cool season to a daytime high of more than 100°F (38°C) in the dry northeast during the hottest months.

Natural Resources

Thailand still has lush forests, fertile soil, and wildlife habitats, though these natural resources have been shrinking in recent years. New efforts are needed to preserve the nation's heritage.

Mist hangs over an already wet rain forest.

The country's rich soil and abundant water supply provide ideal conditions for growing rice. Thailand produces plenty of rice for its people. In addition, it is the world's largest exporter of this food. Mulberry trees, necessary for producing silk, grow abundantly. Rubber plantations are important in the south.

Tin and zinc are mined in Thailand. Other valuable underground resources are copper, potash, limestone, and iron. Rubies and sapphires are mined in the central region, and there are large offshore deposits of natural gas.

Orchards produce a variety of tropical fruits, including pineapples, oranges, grapes, melons, mangoes, papayas, and bananas. In addition, Thailand grows many tropical fruits not often seen in North America. Lansats, rambutans, tamarinds, longans, mangosteens, guavas, jackfruits, and sapodillas are

Monsoons

A monsoon is a wind that blows regularly in certain seasons. The word *monsoon* derives from the Arabic for "season." The summer monsoons in Southeast Asia bring heavy rainfalls. The winds blow clouds over the cool waters of the Indian Ocean, and the air becomes heavy with moisture. Then, as the clouds encounter land, which is warmer than the ocean water, they release rain.

Monsoons are often violent and destructive in other parts of South and Southeast Asia, such as Bangladesh and Vietnam. Thailand, protected by its location, has less frequent severe storms.

Working in rice fields is tedious.

The Phuket Orchid Gardens grow some of the world's most beautiful orchids.

among these sweet treats. One of the most unusual varieties is the durian. It has a tough shell and an unpleasant odor, but a person brave enough to eat it usually likes it— and the durian is very nutritious. For many people, orchids symbolize the beauty and spirit of Thailand. More than one thousand species of orchids grow wild in national parks and other wild areas. Also, they are raised in hundreds of orchid farms and as ornamental plants in Thai gardens. Not surprisingly, Thailand is a world leader in the export of orchids.

Conservation

In the 1940s, a group of people in Thailand formed the nation's first organization concerned about the environment—the Association for the Conservation of Wildlife. Some twenty years later, the government got into the picture. An act to protect wildlife was passed and, beginning in 1961, a few national parks and wildlife preserves were established.

In 1964, the government proclaimed that 40 percent of the country should be kept as forestland. For a variety of reasons, this goal has not yet been reached.

In the 1970s, some Thai students became upset about the widespread poaching of animals. They conducted mass demonstrations and protests. Another issue that caught public attention was a proposal to create a hydroelectric dam across a river in a thickly forested area inhabited by many kinds of wildlife. The project was shelved, proposed again, and defeated again.

Wildlife Fund Thailand was founded in 1983 with strong support from the king and queen. King Bhumibol said, "Thailand has enjoyed a favorable habitat. But it must be preserved so that it will not change from a land of gardens and rice into a desert."

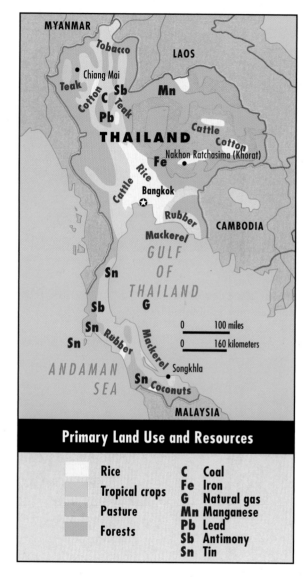

Primary Land Use and Resources

Rice		C	Coal
Tropical crops		Fe	Iron
		G	Natural gas
Pasture		Mn	Manganese
Forests		Pb	Lead
		Sb	Antimony
		Sn	Tin

Phuket Island lies within a national park established by the Thai government.

Thailand has a widespread national park system, but the budget is too small to care for the parks adequately. The nation now has eighty national parks, as well as many wildlife preserves that are closed to the public, and forty-five forest

A Hunter Turned Conservationist

Dr. Boonsong Lekagul, a physician who died in the early 1990s, was one of Thailand's most important conservationists. In his early adult years, he was also known as one of the nation's best hunters.

Dr. Boonsong claimed that he fell in love with animals through the sights of his rifle. But one day in 1959, he became so disgusted with killing that he threw down his gun and never used it again.

Shortly after this experience, Dr. Boonsong met with an officer from the U.S. National Park Service. They toured Thailand together and worked out plans for a national park service. The doctor mapped out the boundaries of Khao Yai, which became Thailand's first national park and is the nation's third-largest park today. He then campaigned hard for legislation to protect his nation's wildlife and its precious natural regions.

preserves. These parks and preserves occupy 13 percent of the nation's total land area.

The growth of industrialization and the needs of agriculture often conflict with protection of the environment. But increased public awareness of the problems may help people to find solutions.

Tourists at the national park Phangnga Bay

Creatures Great and Small

Thailand has more kinds of plant and animal life—
flora and fauna—than almost anywhere else on Earth.
The south has life-forms that thrive in the equatorial
climates of Malaysia and Indonesia. Species that need
a slightly cooler climate live in the far north.

An Indian verditer flycatcher

THAILAND LIES AT THE CROSSROADS of these two habitats. Some of its animals and plants exist nowhere else except in the nearby countries of China and Laos.

This small nation has more species of birds than all of Europe or North America. The long coast along Thailand's peninsula is alive with large coral reefs and hosts of other marine life. Forestlands are homes for many kinds of animals, such as Asia's largest mammal, the elephant, and the world's smallest, the hog-nosed bat. The fields and streams of the plains attract amphibians, reptiles, moths, and butterflies.

Scientists estimate that 10 percent of the world's species of birds can be seen in Thailand, along with 10 percent of the fish, 5 percent of the reptiles, and 3 percent of the amphibians.

Butterflies are protected at the Sainamphung Orchid Nursery and Butterfly Farm near Chiang Mai.

Opposite: **The Regent Chiang Mai Resort**

Elephants are held in high regard in Thailand. Often their images are sculpted into buildings.

Danger Looms

In the past, the rulers of kingdoms often established animal preserves. The purpose was not so much to protect the animals as it was to keep a supply of game for the hunting pleasure of the kings and their courts. Common people were prohibited from killing animals in the royal preserves.

Most kings in Thailand did not have such preserves, but an animal sanctuary was established nearly 800 years ago by King Ramkhamhaeng. Laws protected elephants in his kingdom because of their importance to the nation's economy and the Thai way of life.

Areas surrounding temples were also traditionally safe havens for animals, because Buddhist priests do not believe in killing any living creature. The first official protection of animal life in modern Thai history was the Wild Elephant Protection Act, passed in 1900.

Before the twentieth century, laws to protect plants and animals were unnecessary in Thailand. The population was small, and there was plenty of room for an abundance of both flora and fauna.

In recent decades, however, things have changed greatly and at an alarming rate. With the population boom that followed World War II (1939–1945), more and more forestland was cleared for raising crops. Other forests were destroyed to make room for highways and dams. And, as more people moved into the cities and industries grew, pollution also took its toll. Before World War II, 70 percent of Thailand was forested; today, according to some estimates, the figure may be less than 20 percent.

As the forests shrink, many animals lose their habitats. At least twelve species that once moved freely through the wooded areas are now extinct, about a hundred are classified endangered, and more than a thousand are considered rare.

A deforested landscape in northern Thailand

Elephants and Thailand's Forests

The elephant, a symbol of royalty, is the most admired animal in Thailand. Until recently, hundreds of elephants worked side by side with men in the forests of Thailand. The elephants climbed steep, heavily wooded slopes and picked up huge logs with their trunks and tusks. Then they carried the loads down to the riverfronts to be floated to mills.

Teak is a very heavy, valuable wood. Mountains covered with teak trees were one of the country's most valuable natural resources, making logging a major industry. But in 1988, disaster struck. Heavy rains caused a landslide in a region where the lower slopes had been cleared of trees. Hundreds of tons of cut timber thundered down the hillsides, burying villages in the path of the landslide. More than a hundred people were killed.

Recognizing that overcutting the forests was a serious problem, the government brought timber-cutting to a complete standstill. Programs to replant forests have been stepped up.

Thus, many elephants have lost their jobs as beasts of burden in the forest industry. But elephant training still goes on. The Thai people are very fond of these big, gentle creatures. They enjoy watching trained elephants perform in shows at outdoor restaurants and arenas. They travel to places where they can take rides through dense forests on the backs of elephants.

Elephant trainers, called *mahouts*, usually start to work with young elephants while they are still quite young themselves. The trainer and his animal learn skills and stunts as they grow up together.

The Kao Sok National Park

Protected Areas

Most of Thailand's remaining forestland and wildlife now lie within national parks and wildlife sanctuaries. The Wild Animals Reservation and Protection Act of 1960 was the first national law for the protection of wild animals in general. The act established sanctuaries and other areas where hunting is prohibited. Except for scientists doing research, people are forbidden to visit the sanctuaries. The act also named nine species for total protection: the wild water buffalo, the kouprey (a short-haired ox), the serow (a type of longhaired goat), the goral (a member of the goat family), two types of rhinoceros, and three species of deer. Unfortunately, the law was too little and too late; some of these creatures are almost certainly already extinct.

The national parks are popular tourist attractions. Young people who live in the cities—especially Bangkok—love to get away from the noise, the crowds, and the pollution of their everyday lives. They hike in the woods, relax beside beautiful waterfalls, breathe pure air, and enjoy an occasional glimpse of monkeys, deer, and brightly colored tropical birds.

Nearly 12 million people per year were visiting the parks by the late 1990s. About half of these were from Bangkok. Twenty years earlier, only about 1 million people visited the parks.

This increased popularity brings both good news and bad news. The bad news is that more visitors mean more damage to the environment through poaching (illegal hunting), fires,

Thailand's wildlife parks protect the endangered water buffalo.

and pressures to clear more land for recreational use. The good news is that the additional visitors bring increased revenues to Thailand, and return home with a heightened appreciation for the value—and the fragility—of the wild lands and a willingness to work for more and better conservation programs.

The Forests

About two-thirds of the forests in Thailand are made up of deciduous trees that change with the seasons. The remainder are evergreens. Often the two types are found together.

In the wonderful rain forests of Thailand's southern peninsula, the trees are almost all evergreen. They grow in low-lying areas that do not have a dry season. The rain forests are the

Rain forests in low-lying areas never have a dry season.

world's richest ecosystems; they have the greatest variety of types of trees and other plants. Large mammals do not live in rain forests, as there is not enough food for them. Smaller animals and many kinds of birds, however, flourish in that environment.

Evergreen and mixed forests grow at higher altitudes in areas that have a rainy season. The forest floor in these areas gets more light than in rain forests, so there are more shrubs, grasses, and herbs. Savanna forests are more open, with a variety of grasses growing on their plains. These habitats have food to support larger mammals.

Phangnga Bay National Park has limestone mountains as well as mangroves.

Mangrove forests are swampy coastal areas that provide breeding grounds for fish and shellfish. Unfortunately, much of this type of forest in Thailand has been destroyed.

Forests that grow on steep limestone formations are the favorite habitat of the serow, a long-legged goat that does well in this terrain.

Dusit Zoo

A popular spot for families to visit in Bangkok is Dusit Zoo. It is also called *Khao Din*, meaning "Mountain of Earth." Visitors can rent boats and view the animals from a lake in the park. The park has a fine collection of Southeast Asia's wildlife, including gibbons, orangutans, and snakes.

An unusual collection of white (albino) elephants is an important and popular attraction at the zoo. Every white elephant found in Thailand is, by tradition, the property of the king. Throughout Southeast Asia, white elephants have been a royal symbol and appear in Buddhist literature.

The expression "white elephant" has come to mean an unwanted object because kings, long ago, sometimes gave them to people who could not afford to keep them. The kings did this in the hope that the person receiving this gift would go broke trying to care for the animal.

Other animal parks in the vicinity of Bangkok are a snake farm on Rama IV Road; an elephant zoo in Nakhon Pathom province, about 19 miles (30 km) west of the city; and a tiger zoo in Thonburi.

Wildlife

Opposite: **A fishing village in Panyi**

Today, Thailand has between two and three thousand wild elephants and close to five thousand domesticated ones. This is less than half as many as there were in northern Thailand one hundred years ago. Other endangered large animals are bears, tigers, and leopards. Some kinds of deer are still fairly common. Gibbons and monkeys survive in a few protected areas.

Bird-watchers in Thailand have listed nearly a thousand different species. Scientists believe that many more may be discovered in the future. They range from tiny warblers to

A colorful peafowl

A Visit to Tarutao National Park

Tarutao National Park, Thailand's first marine park, is on and around a group of romantically beautiful tropical islands in the Strait of Malacca of the Andaman Sea. Visitors get there by boat from a harbor near Thailand's southern boundary. They stay in government bungalows or in campgrounds.

Tarutao, the largest island, is a place of mystery and melodrama. Old legends tell of a curse placed on the islands by a long-ago Malay princess. For centuries, pirates used Tarutao as a base for raids on merchant ships. It was also a prison colony for a short time.

About five hundred people live on one of the islands.

They live by fishing and farming and earn extra income selling seashells to tourists.

Mountain ranges covered with scrub and mangrove forests have nature trails that lead to magnificent views of the islands and the sparkling waters. The wide, white beaches are often bordered by wildflowers, and waterfalls and caves add drama to the landscape.

Colorful fish and coral reefs attract snorkelers and scuba divers. Dolphins, sea turtles (below), and even whales swim offshore. More than a hundred species of birds on the islands include terns, ospreys, egrets, hornbills, hawks, and doves.

majestic cranes, wise-faced owls, and splendid peacocks. They come in brilliant shades of yellow, orange, red, blue, and green.

Migrant birds find breeding grounds in Thailand as they travel between their summer and winter homes. Forest birds are more numerous than waterbirds, but ducks, cormorants, egrets, and herons inhabit marshes, lakes, ponds, rivers, and mangrove swamps.

Some three hundred kinds of fish are caught on both sides of the peninsula in southern Thailand. Sportfishers find marlin, sailfish, and several kinds of sharks. Four kinds of turtles nest on the islands, and large stretches of coral reef are a habitat for hundreds of fish species.

Yesterday and Today

Thousands of years ago, nomadic people roamed throughout Southeast Asia. Over many centuries, they learned to farm. They made metal tools, caught fish, raised animals, and grew rice and other foods. Some cave drawings of people and animals found in northeastern Thailand are at least three or four thousand years old.

Much later, small kingdoms developed in Southeast Asia. Part of what is now northeastern Thailand was under the influence of the Khmer Empire.

The capital of the Khmer Empire was Angkor Wat, in present-day Cambodia. Today, Angkor Wat is world-famous, an ancient city filled with magnificent temples. Not quite as well known, but equally important and similar in architecture, are the ancient wats in northeastern Thailand. Thailand's Fine Arts Department started restoring some of these world treasures in the 1960s.

The Golden Age

Sukhothai means "dawn of happiness." Sukhothai was also the dawn of Thailand's recorded history—it was the first Thai kingdom. Nearly eight hundred years ago, Thai chiefs grew tired of Khmer rule and rose up in revolt. One of the chiefs, Si Inthtrahit, established a kingdom and capital city, both named Sukhothai, in the year 1238. The Sukhothai period is remembered as a Golden Age.

The Buddha sits prominently at the Wat Mahathat in Sukhothai Historical Park.

Opposite: **A painting depicting early life in Thailand**

Prasat Phimai

One of the first Khmer temples to be restored, and one of the most important, is Prasat Phimai, about 37 miles (60 km) northeast of the city of Khorat. Originally a walled city, Prasat Phimai was built mainly of red and white sandstone. Two rivers formed a boundary on three sides of the compound. Outer and inner *gopuras* (pavilions) on each of the four sides surround the main temple. Many modern Thai *prangs* (sacred buildings honoring Buddha) show the influence of Khmer architecture. The shape is described by different observers as similar to a pinecone or a corncob.

On weekends and holidays, Prasat Phimai is crowded with families and young people from Bangkok and other parts of Thailand. The visitors are proud of the work their government is doing to preserve Thailand's religious and cultural heritage.

Si Inthtrahit's son, King Ramkhamhaeng, was a remarkable man. He did not demand taxes from his people. The kingdom was prosperous, with enough food for all. The king encouraged people to bring their problems and disputes directly to him. He promised to treat everyone fairly and justly. A devout Buddhist, King Ramkhamhaeng built many monasteries.

Trade with other kingdoms flourished. Local artisans made beautiful glazed ceramic pieces for export. A written script for the Thai language was developed during this period. Some historians believe the king himself may have invented it.

The kingdom of Sukhothai lasted for a little more than a hundred years. During that same time, other small kingdoms to the south were growing stronger.

Ayutthaya

The kingdom of Ayutthaya took control of Sukhothai in 1350. It was the economic and cultural center of the Thai people for the next four centuries. The capital, also named Ayutthaya, was one of the finest cities in Asia. Canals and waterways provided transportation throughout a beautiful metropolis adorned with monasteries. Vast fertile rice fields surrounded the city.

For a short time, Ayutthaya expanded as far as the Khmer capital of Angkor. The kingdom, however, became too big to be ruled with the personal attention King Ramkhamhaeng had given to Sukhothai. So a governmental bureaucracy developed.

The Buddhist temple of Wat Chai Mongkol at Ayutthaya

Everything was not always peaceful. Wars frequently broke out with neighboring countries, especially with Burma. The Burmese conquered Ayutthaya and ruled the kingdom from 1569 to 1590.

Free of Burmese rule after 1590, Ayutthaya became prosperous. The kingdom sold its surplus of rice, dried fish, and forest products to other lands.

International trade grew—not only with Asian neighbors but with Arab and European merchants as well.

In 1767, Burmese troops invaded Ayutthaya again and destroyed the city. Thousands of Thais were killed and captured before a military leader emerged. Phraya Taksin, half Thai and half Chinese, defeated both the Burmese invaders and local rivals. He declared himself King Taksin.

Many Buddhist monks visit the Wat Arun Temple of Dawn in Thonburi.

Thonburi

Ayutthaya was a ruined city, so King Taksin established a new capital at Thonburi, a village on the west side of the Chao Phraya River. He was successful in keeping Burmese invaders out. He also reestablished international trade and encouraged literature, the arts, and Buddhism.

Taksin also had enemies, some of whom thought he was a religious fanatic. In 1782, he was deposed and executed. In present-day Thailand, however, he is remembered for his accomplishments and known as Taksin the Great.

Bangkok

A general, Chao Phraya Chakri, was chosen to succeed Taksin. He was the first king in the Chakri Dynasty. All of Thailand's kings since then have been members of the Royal House of Chakri. They hold the royal title of Rama. The general was named Rama I; the present king is Rama IX.

The history of Thailand is largely the story of its kings. They have been a group of remarkable men—well educated and wise men who were dedicated to helping their people. Through the centuries, they have kept their nation united and free from foreign domination.

Rama I

Rama I established Bangkok as his capital and created an island city with a system of canals connecting to the Chao Phraya River. He wanted to build a city as magnificent as Ayutthaya had been. The Grand Palace, the Temple of the Emerald Buddha, and several Ayutthaya-style monasteries were constructed during his reign.

Wat Phra Keo is one of Thailand's most famous Buddhist shrines.

The Chakri Dynasty

Rama I	Chao Phraya Chakri	1782–1809
Rama II	Isarasuntorn	1809–1824
Rama III	Chetsadabodin	1824–1851
Rama IV	Mongkut	1851–1868
Rama V	Chulalongkorn	1868–1910
Rama VI	Vajiravudh	1910–1925
Rama VII	Prajadhipok	1925–1935
Rama VIII	Ananda Mahidol*	1935–1946
Rama IX	Bhumibol Adulyadej	1946–

*A regent ruled for the prince 1935–1945

Rama I also expanded the territories of his nation, then named Siam. Several attacks by the Burmese were repelled, and the region of Chiang Mai joined Siam. Rama I also promoted literature, the arts, and devotion to Buddhism.

Siam enjoyed a period of stability and cultural development under the next two kings. Western powers were too busy with wars in Europe to pay much attention to Asia.

Mongkut, with one of his wives

Rama IV

Prince Mongkut, who was to become Rama IV, spent his early years as a monk, studying Buddhist scriptures. His intellectual curiosity went far beyond religion, however. He learned Latin and English, and he was a scholar of Western geography and culture, as well as of science.

Heroine of Khorat

One brief disturbance interrupted the serenity of Rama III's reign. Prince Anu of Vientiane (in Laos) led an invasion of Khorat, took over the city, and threatened to make slaves of the citizens. When the prince left Khorat to lead an attack elsewhere, the wife of a local official decided to fight back.

Tao Suranari, also known as Khunying Mo, got together with some other women and threw a party for the Laotian soldiers. First they got the men drunk; then they killed them. The Laotian prince was defeated.

Today, a large statue of Tao Suranari stands in the city square in Khorat surrounded by a spacious platform. Local people bring offerings of flowers, small toys, and food and place them in front of the statue in the hope that the heroine's spirit will grant them special protection. If their wishes are granted, the supplicants often hire a quartet of folksingers to perform a traditional Khorat folk song in appreciation.

While he was king, Mongkut faced the threat of foreign domination. The British Empire was expanding and taking over several neighboring countries. King Mongkut avoided this fate for Thailand by negotiating trade treaties with several European countries. He also welcomed Western advisers to Thailand to help him make reforms in administration and technology.

King Chulalongkorn (Rama V) and his son, Crown Prince Vajiravudh

King Chulalongkorn

King Mongkut's son Chulalongkorn was only sixteen when he became Rama V. He ruled Thailand for forty-two years. They were years of great accomplishment.

Kings of Thailand, as in many other countries, had absolute power. They made the laws, collected the taxes, and decided when to send their soldiers to war. In

The Museum of Currency was once the home of King Chulalongkorn's son.

addition, early kings were regarded almost as gods. Mongkut and Chulalongkorn, while still holding onto absolute rule, were close to their people. They traveled widely throughout the country and learned about their people firsthand. Their reforms did much to improve life for the citizens.

Chulalongkorn visited neighboring nations and made two long trips to Europe. He was the first Siamese king to do this. He wanted to learn from other countries without becoming dominated or sacrificing Thai traditions and values.

One of his first reforms was to abolish slavery. He built railroads and provided postal and telegraph services to the provinces. He reorganized and modernized national and provincial administrations. Before this time, all childhood education was in the hands of the monks. King Chulalongkorn established public schools and health centers. He arranged for a number of Thai students to go abroad for part of their education.

Like his father, King Rama V practiced careful diplomacy with foreign powers in order to avoid becoming a colony of Europe. In spite of these efforts, he found it necessary to surrender Siamese territories in Indochina to France in 1893 and 1904. And, in 1907, Siam ceded claims to Malay states to Britain.

A Period of Turmoil

King Chulalongkorn's son Vajiravudh, Rama VI, was educated at Harrow School and Oxford University in England. He was an enthusiastic nationalist and much interested in military affairs. He decided to send Thai soldiers to Europe to fight with the Allies in World War I (1914–1918). This decision increased the stature of Siam among foreign nations. After the war, Siam became a founding member of the League of Nations.

Vajiravudh was also a poet, playwright, and reformer. He passed a law making education compulsory. He founded an English-style boys' boarding school in Thailand, and

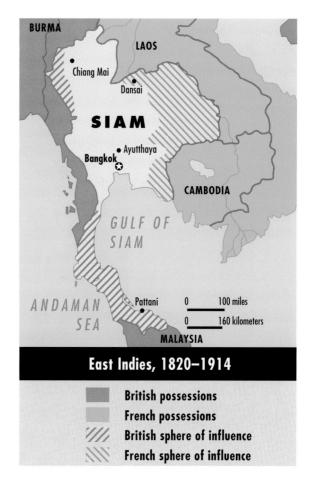

East Indies, 1820–1914

- ■ British possessions
- ■ French possessions
- ▨ British sphere of influence
- ▧ French sphere of influence

King Vajiravudh (Rama VI)

established Chulalongkorn University. Family names had not been used in Thailand before this time, but Rama VI decreed that all citizens should adopt and use family names, as Westerners do. Thais generally identify themselves and one another, however, by their first names.

Prajadhipok, the younger brother of Vajiravudh, succeeded him on the throne in 1925 as Rama VII. Prajadhipok's reign included a period of upheaval, marked by a worldwide depression and a growing desire in Siam for a liberal constitutional government. Although he was sympathetic to this idea, Prajadhipok was unable to bring various factions together.

In 1932, a group of civil servants and army officers seized control of the government. It was a bloodless coup d'état that replaced the 700-year-old absolute monarchy with a constitutional monarchy. Different groups then struggled to gain control of the government. Believing he could not work effectively with either group, King Prajadhipok abdicated in 1935. The government then elected one of his nephews, ten-year-old Prince Ananda Mahidol, to be the next king. A Council of Regents ruled for the prince until 1945.

Phibun Songkhram, a military officer, led the country from 1938 until 1945. He came back to power in 1947 and suspended the 1932 constitution. A few years later, he abolished the constitution altogether. Phibun continued to be an important force in the government until his death sixteen years later.

In 1939, the government officially changed the name of the country to Prathet Thai, or Thailand in English. The name has two interpretations. The Sanskrit words mean "land of the free," the popular meaning. In addition, the major ethnic group of the region has always been called Tai. In either case,

Prince Ananda Mahidol, heir to the Siamese throne, ruled for one year as Rama VIII

Thailand is an appropriate name for the country and its citizens alike. The name was changed back to Siam for a short time, but since 1949, it has been Thailand.

In 1945, the young King Ananda ascended to the throne. Only a year later, he was found shot to death in his bedroom. The details of his death remain a mystery. His younger brother, Prince Bhumibol Adulyadej, was proclaimed King Rama IX on the same day, beginning the longest reign by any Thai king in history.

A Constitutional Monarchy

"I shall advise my son Vajiravudh to present a gift to the citizens immediately as he ascends the throne. I mean to give them the parliament and constitution."

THE YEAR WAS 1910, AND KING CHULALONGKORN was speaking to his government ministers. He had been the absolute monarch of Siam, as Thailand was called then, for forty-two years. He had reigned with compassion and wisdom, and the people loved him. Chulalongkorn had vision, and he believed it was time for his subjects to begin to govern themselves.

King Chulalongkorn died later that year, and Vajiravudh became Rama VI. He was sympathetic to the idea of establishing a constitution and parliament, but he was occupied with international affairs and World War I. He never got around to establishing a constitutional government.

Prince Prajadhipok succeeded his brother on the throne as Rama VII. He had not expected to become king and was not experienced in political matters. He gave some thought to the question of a constitution, but matters were taken out of his hands before he could act.

A group of intellectual leaders, supported by the military, formed the People's Party. In 1932, they sent a message to the king, informing him that they were taking over the govern-

King Prajadhipok (Rama VII)

Opposite: **Government head-quarters in Bangkok**

ment. He would be allowed to stay on as king, but the power would pass to new leadership.

King Prajadhipok agreed to the new arrangement, "for the sake of peace and in order to save useless bloodshed and to avoid confusion and loss to the country." He also stated that he had already considered making the change himself. He signed the new constitution on December 10, 1932. The constitution has been rewritten several times since then, most recently in 1997.

In Thailand's constitutional monarchy, the king is named the head of the armed forces and the upholder of all religions. Laws are enacted by the Parliament. The Council of Ministers, also called the Cabinet, headed by the prime minister, runs the

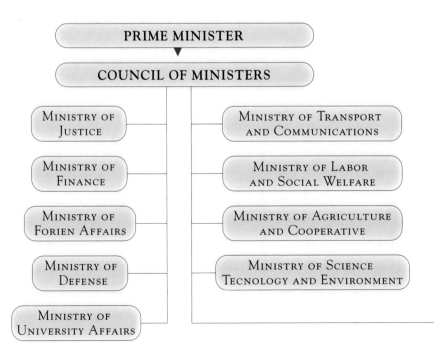

PRIME MINISTER

COUNCIL OF MINISTERS

MINISTRY OF JUSTICE

MINISTRY OF FINANCE

MINISTRY OF FORIEN AFFAIRS

MINISTRY OF DEFENSE

MINISTRY OF UNIVERSITY AFFAIRS

MINISTRY OF TRANSPORT AND COMMUNICATIONS

MINISTRY OF LABOR AND SOCIAL WELFARE

MINISTRY OF AGRICULTURE AND COOPERATIVE

MINISTRY OF SCIENCE TECNOLOGY AND ENVIRONMENT

Government building in Bangkok

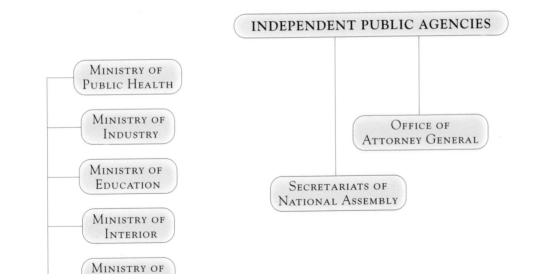

INDEPENDENT PUBLIC AGENCIES

MINISTRY OF PUBLIC HEALTH

MINISTRY OF INDUSTRY

MINISTRY OF EDUCATION

MINISTRY OF INTERIOR

MINISTRY OF COMMERCE

OFFICE OF ATTORNEY GENERAL

SECRETARIATS OF NATIONAL ASSEMBLY

National Symbols

In every village and town in Thailand, the national flag is raised each day at 8:00 A.M. and lowered at 6:00 P.M. The national anthem is played during these ceremonies.

The flag has five horizontal stripes. From top to bottom, the colors are red, white, blue, white, and red. The red stripes stand for the nation and the white ones for religion. The wider blue band in the center, occupying one-third of the total area, symbolizes the monarchy. These three concepts—nation, religion, and monarchy—unite the Thai people.

This flag was adopted by King Rama VI in 1917. An earlier one pictured a white elephant against a red background.

The national and royal symbol is the *garuda*, a mythical creature that is half bird and half man. The Hindu god Vishnu used the garuda for transportation. The

garuda insignia is widely used in Southeast Asia. The king of Thailand can honor a company that has made outstanding economic or charitable contributions by giving them permission to use this emblem as evidence of royal approval.

day-to-day business of government. There are fourteen cabinet ministries: Defense; Finance; Foreign Affairs; Agriculture and Cooperatives; Transport and Communications; Commerce; Interior; Justice; Labor and Social Welfare; Science, Technology, and Environment; Education; Public Health; Industry; and University Affairs. A bureaucracy of hundreds of thousands of civil servants is employed by these ministries.

Courts fall under the jurisdiction of the Ministry of Justice. They are divided into three levels. Legal matters are first heard by one of about 140 courts of first instance, located throughout the kingdom. There are four courts of appeal and one supreme court.

National and Royal Anthems

The music of the Thai national anthem was composed in 1932 by Professor Phra Jenduriyang and its lyrics were written in 1939 by Colonel Luang Saranuprabhandi.

Thailand is the unity of Thai blood and body.
The whole country belongs to the Thai people,
maintaining thus far for the Thai.
All Thais intend to unite together.
Thais love peace but do not fear to fight.
They will never let anyone threaten their independence.
They will sacrifice every drop of their blood to contribute to the nation, will serve their country with pride and prestige full of victory.
CHAI YO. [Cheers].

A special anthem honoring the king is played on many public occasions to express the respect and love that the Thai people have for their monarch.

We, Your Majesty's loyal subjects,
Pay homage with deep-felt veneration,
To the supreme Protector of the Realm,
The mightiest of monarchs complete with transcendent virtues,
Under whose benevolent rule, we, Your subjects,
Receive protection and happiness,
Prosperity and peace;
And we wish that whatsoever Your Majesty may desire,
The same may be fulfilled.

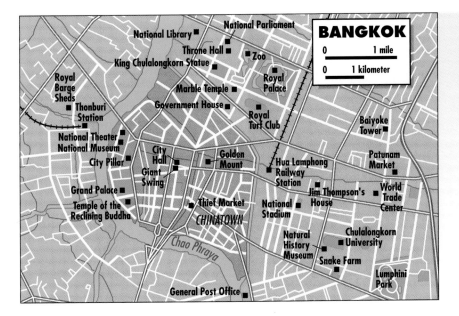

Bangkok: Did You Know This?

Population: 5,620,591
Founded: 1782
Meaning of name: Village of wild plums
Area: 604 square miles (1,565 sq km)
Average Daily Temperature: 86°F (30°C) in April; and 77°F (25°C) in December
Average Annual Rainfall: 60 inches (152 cm)

The National Assembly

Laws are written and adopted by the two houses of the Thai Parliament, or National Assembly. Members of the House of Representatives are elected by the people for four-year terms. In the Senate, members are appointed by the king on recommendation of the Cabinet. They serve for six years.

Military Service

Career military men in Thailand hold leadership positions in government and industry. For several decades, most of the nation's prime ministers have been military officers. Several ministries have also been headed by military officials. In addition, career soldiers sit on the boards of many financial and industrial institutions. Both military personnel and civil servants are well paid and enjoy a high degree of prestige.

There are three branches of service: the Royal Thai Army, Royal Thai Navy, and Royal Thai Air Force. Every young man in Thailand is required to spend two years in military service beginning at age twenty or, if he is still in school, after graduation.

The Thai military

A royal statue in a Bangkok square

Local Government

Thailand is divided into seventy-six provinces, each with a capital city. A governor heads up each provincial government. The provinces have three levels of local government—the village, the *tambon* (group of villages), and the district. Villages are self-governing, with an elected *phu-yai-ban* as the administrator. Until 1983, this administrator was always male; since 1983, women have also been able to run for election to the position. The candidate must be literate, at least twenty-five years old, and must have lived in the village for at least six months.

The phu-yai-ban keeps the village records and acts as a mediator in minor disputes. He or she is also the village spokesperson in dealing with the national government.

From two to twenty-eight villages are organized into a tambon. There are nearly five thousand tambons in Thailand. They are administered by committees made up of local leaders such as a school administrator, an agricultural extension worker, and a health worker. Two or more additional committee members are selected by the district officer. These committees make decisions about roads, budgets, and other matters concerning the member villages.

The royal family at the fiftieth anniversary of the coronation of Rama IX

Many Governments, One King

The government has changed hands many times since King Bhumibol ascended to the throne in 1946. Some of the changes have been peaceful, while others have involved military force and bloodshed. A new constitution has been written nearly every time the political power has shifted from one faction to another—more than sixteen times!

Through all the turmoil and struggle among rival political groups, King Bhumibol has been the one constant factor. Throughout the more than fifty years of his reign, the Thai people

Bhumibol Adulyadej

Rama IX

1927   Born December 5 in Cambridge, Massachusetts, where his father was
        studying medicine
1946   Declared king when his older brother died
1950   Married Mom Rajawongse Sirikit Kitiyakara; crowned a week later at the
        Grand Palace, Bangkok
1951   Birth of Princess Ubolratana
1952   Birth of Crown Prince Maha Vajiralongkorn
1955   Birth of Princess Maha Chakri Sirindhorn
1957   Birth of Princess Chulabhorn
1996   Golden Jubilee Year—national celebration of king's fifty-year reign

have been united in their respect and love for him and Queen
Sirikit. Their pictures hang in nearly every home and office
in Thailand. They are welcomed by their people wherever
they appear.

King Bhumibol has encouraged all efforts to protect and
promote democracy. Although he has no direct power over
the three branches of government, he is expected to voice his
opinion on state affairs and to speak out for the good of the
people. He is a diplomatic leader. More than once, he has
avoided a national crisis by persuading political opponents to
meet and cooperate with one another.

The king is a multitalented man. He speaks three languages besides Thai, plays the saxophone and composes jazz,
and is a painter, sculptor, and photographer. He is also an
award-winning sailor, a mathematician, an engineer, and an
inventor.

The Thai royal family poses with U.S. president Bill Clinton and his wife, Hillary, under the portrait of the king's grandfather, King Chulalongkorn, at Bangkok's Grand Palace.

Above all, the king and queen are admired for the many projects they have undertaken to improve conditions for the Thai people. King Bhumibol has traveled to every one of Thailand's seventy-six provinces and met personally with the people.

When the king and queen are in Bangkok, the royal residence is Chitralada Villa of Dusit Palace, a gracious estate, but much more modest than the Grand Palace where their predecessors lived. The royal family also has four residences in other

parts of the country. One is in the north, one in the northeast, one on the Gulf of Thailand, and one in the south. These homes give them a chance to know all of the nation well.

King Bhumibol is involved in hundreds of projects that affect his people. He is sensitive to local needs, such as building a new temple, as well as to long-range national programs with far-reaching benefits. He heads foundations that fund new projects or provide disaster relief.

The Queen Sirikit Botanical Garden

The grounds of Chitralada Villa are used for agricultural research and experimentation. There, rice fields, a dairy farm, fish ponds, and a milk-processing plant are designed to find ways to improve life for farmers.

During King Bhumibol's reign, the rural areas, where four out of five Thais live, have enjoyed tremendous improvements in transportation and communication. Many new roads and railroads have been built, and postal and telegraph services now reach all regions of the country. And nearly every Thai home has a television set today.

In the past, the major crop grown in the far northern part of Thailand was poppies. This region, known as the Golden Triangle, included parts of Myanmar and Laos as well as Thailand. Nomadic hill tribes grew the poppies to supply the international drug trade with raw opium. King Bhumibol has done a great deal to convince the tribal people to plant other crops, such as coffee, flowers, and fruit trees. In the long run, these crops are more lucrative. The poppy growers were paid very little for their part in the hugely profitable narcotics industry.

The agricultural changes also encouraged the tribes to stop moving about and to settle in villages. Educational and health-care facilities spearheaded by royal projects were added incentives.

Environmental protection and conservation are major interests of the king. He has been influential in legislation that preserves national parks, forests, and wetlands, and he has also promoted ambitious reforestation programs.

King Bhumibol, a devout Buddhist, has spent time as a monk, like many other Thai men. In addition, the constitution declares him to be the "upholder of all religions." In this capacity, he visits mosques in the south, where a number of Muslims live. He also brings different religious groups together to promote their understanding of one another.

On the fiftieth anniversary of his coronation, King Bhumibol presents gifts to attending Buddhist monks.

The king presides over many ceremonial functions and state occasions. He greets foreign dignitaries who visit Thailand. And he personally presents diplomas to many graduates of universities and military colleges.

Queen Sirikit is as involved with projects as her husband is. Among other things, she works directly with rural women, setting up training centers and helping develop handicraft industries. She is also a key member of the World Wildlife Fund (Thailand), which works to protect endangered animals.

Both the king and queen are committed to living the words he spoke during his coronation: "We shall rule in righteousness for the benefit of the people."

Thailand has had a history of many changes in its national constitution and administration since 1932. Most of these changes, however, have been peaceful. To a great extent, this nation has been more politically stable than many other developing countries have, and its people have been more free to run their own affairs. Loyalty to the monarchy and freedom of the press keep the people hopeful for a more perfect democracy.

Opposite: **Queen Rajawongse Sirikit Kitiyakara**

Earning a Living

Timber in the forests, minerals in the ground, rice in the fields, and fish in the waters. The riches of old Siam lured traders to the port city of Ayutthaya some five hundred years ago. The Chinese were first, followed by the Europeans, Japanese, Persians, and Arabs. The kings and aristocrats of the kingdom amassed great wealth from trade.

THEN THE EUROPEAN TRADERS LOST INTEREST IN THIS corner of the world. They preferred to deal with the East Indies and Singapore.

Opposite: **A fisher on the Mekong River**

The economy of Siam became increasingly dependent on rice. By the early part of the twentieth century, four of every five people in the nation earned a living from raising or trading rice. The nation was the chief supplier of rice for much of Asia.

Meanwhile, neighboring countries ruled by Europeans were developing industry. As independent governments replaced the colonial rulers, they inherited modern businesses

Most Thai farmers still use buffalo to plow their rice fields.

with factories and many educated workers. At the end of World War II, Thailand found itself far behind Burma (as Myanmar was still called), Malaysia, Indochina, and the Philippines in industrial development.

In the years after the war, local entrepreneurs in Thailand started small businesses, and a number of them were very successful. Additional lands were cleared for rice cultivation, and new farms were created. Thailand's economy grew steadily. With the help of the United States, dams were built to provide irrigation stations. Transportation became easier as new roads were built, making it easier to get farm goods to market. In 1960, 80 percent of Thailand's exports were products of the farms, fisheries, and forests.

Banks and other businesses prospered as the agricultural economy grew. Business owners were anxious to expand the small manufacturing sector and produce non-agricultural goods for export.

A dried-fish seller carts goods to market on a specially made motorbike.

What Thailand Grows, Makes, and Mines

Agriculture

Sugarcane	54,616,000 metric tons
Rice	19,950,000 metric tons
Tapioca	17,340,000 metric tons

Manufacturing

Cement	26,300,000 metric tons
Refined sugar	3,650,500 metric tons
Chemical fertilizer	458,103 metric tons

Mining

Limestone	42,224,000 metric tons
Gypsum	8,140,000 metric tons
Kaolin clay	417,000 metric tons

Recession, to Boom, to Crash

In 1984–1985, a major recession slowed down Thailand's economy. Very rapidly, Thailand was swept up in the global economy.

Multinational companies such as Coca-Cola, Exxon, Hilton, and McDonald's appeared on Thailand's business scene. Investors from Japan, Hong Kong, and Taiwan brought factories to the Bangkok area, where they could find cheaper labor. In a short time, exports of textiles and other inexpensive manufactured goods were overtaking rice. Computer parts and other electronic items soon joined the stream of goods flowing out of Thai ports.

A new class of merchants and business tycoons—Thailand's newly rich—was making fortunes. For more than ten years, the

Thai Money

The basic money unit in Thailand is the baht (B). Paper money is made in amounts of 10, 20, 50, 100, 500, and 1,000 baht. Coins are 1-, 5-, and 10-baht pieces. The king's face is shown on the front of every coin and every bill. The Grand Palace is on the reverse side of coins.

Each denomination of paper currency is a different color. The 10 B note is brown, 20 B green, 50 B blue, 100 B red, 500 B purple, and 1,000 B beige. Various traditional symbols are used as decorations, such as the royal coat of arms, the lotus flower, and the national emblem. The garuda, the mythical man-bird, is part of the national emblem.

A special royal commemorative emblem appears on the front of the 500 B bill. It was designed and officially adopted to celebrate King Bhumibol's Golden Jubilee in 1996—the fiftieth anniversary of his reign.

Important historical persons and events are commemorated on the back of bills. For example, Kings Rama I and Rama II appear on the back of the 500 B bill, along with a picture of the Royal Palace. Rama VII, his seal, and the Hall of Assembly are on the 50 B bill, and King Taksin on the 20 B.

The 100 B bill honors Rama V and Rama VI and their influence on education. A book and a candle symbolize knowledge. Some children are shown in a modern classroom; others are being taught by monks, who were the first teachers in Thailand.

---

nation's economy boomed. Between 1985 and 1994, it reached first place among world nations in economic growth, according to the World Bank. From 1991 to 1995, exports doubled in value, from $28.8 billion (in U.S. dollars) to $56.4 billion.

In 1995, Thailand's top ten exports, in value, were computers and parts, garments, rubber, integrated circuits, footwear and parts, gems and jewelry, plastic products, frozen prawns, rice, and canned seafood.

Thai government ministries were projecting that the nation's economy would double in size by the year 2000, and the World Bank predicted this would be the world's eighth-largest economy by 2020.

Opposite: **A modern shopping center in Bangkok**

Then came a new crisis. In 1997, the devaluing of the Thai currency resulted in rapid inflation, and Asian stock markets became unstable. Many people lost fortunes overnight.

What the future will bring is yet to be seen. Many industrial workers have returned to the countryside, hoping that agriculture will again help them to make ends meet.

Many young people work in factories in large cities.

How the Boom Changed Thailand

Thailand's ten-year boom brought many changes. Industry became a much larger part of the economy than agriculture. The factories needed workers. Young people left rural areas to live and work in the cities—mostly Bangkok.

At first, the big increase was in manufactured goods that depended on cheap, largely unskilled labor, such as clothing and footwear. At that time, most of the villagers had only four years of schooling, which had usually been enough to prepare them for jobs in agriculture. Soon, however, technological industries needed more highly skilled workers.

Thailand's educational system was not geared to technology. Even the institutions of higher education were not preparing students for work as technicians and scientists—they were turning out administrators and bureaucrats. The government tried to meet this challenge with crash programs to increase the number of years children spent in public schools. Extension courses for adults were also set up. These measures were not fast enough to meet the need, however, so the businesses began to recruit employees from other countries.

Before the boom, manufacturing in Thailand was done mostly in small, individually owned factories. Owners and employees often lived in apartments above the business, in shop houses. As the economy grew, companies became larger and larger, and relationships between workers and bosses became less close. The gap grew wider between those who were getting rich in this new society and those who worked for low wages.

Beautiful resorts line Thailand's coasts.

The look of the land changed, too. Thousands of acres of agricultural land were gobbled up for other uses—industrial parks, housing projects, resorts, and golf courses. The tourism boom that began in the 1970s was in part responsible. Travelers from Asian and Pacific countries discovered the historical and natural treasures of Thailand. As a result, resorts and other facilities to

support the new tourist industry were built. Bangkok sprawled out into the countryside. New industrial centers began to appear in communities 50 miles (80 km) out of Bangkok. Then new regional centers appeared near other main cities—Chiang Mai, Khorat, Khon Kaen. In one generation, Thailand's forests shrank by half.

Downtown Bangkok

Many young people who had moved to the cities came back to their villages after only five years or so. They wanted to get away from the bad air, traffic, unpleasant living conditions, and stress of urban life. Some of them started small businesses back home.

The Future

What happens next? That is a question only time can answer. One thing is certain: Thailand is now part of the global economy. What happens in Thailand has an effect on other nations, especially its Asian neighbors. It will take international cooperation to bring more stability to developing countries. At the same time, the people and government of Thailand must find their own answers to the social problems resulting from the rapid economic changes of recent years.

Meet the Thai People

Archaeologists have recently learned that people living in several regions of present-day Thailand knew how to cast metal and make pottery as long ago as 2000 B.C. Formerly, most scholars had believed that the ancestors of present-day Thai people originated in China and migrated south from there only about thirteen hundred years ago. Now it seems that there were highly developed civilizations in this region well before those later migrations.

Previous page:
**An artist painting pottery
at the Sankampaeng Kilns**

**Hmong women in traditional
New Year's clothing**

THAILAND HAS A FAIRLY HOMOGENEOUS POPULATION. MOST of its more than 60 million people share the same ethnic heritage and the same religion. It was once estimated that nearly 80 percent of the people are ethnic Thais and 95 percent are Buddhists. However, large numbers of people from neighboring countries—refugees and workers recruited to work in Thailand—have recently increased the total population and changed the mix. Accurate and up-to-date counts are not presently available.

About 12 percent are of Chinese descent, most of them second or third generation. These children and grandchil-

dren of immigrants from China grew up speaking Thai and think of Thailand as their native country. Intermarriage is common, which results in a blurring of ethnic differences.

About another 3.7 percent are Malays. The majority of the Malay people live in the south, near the Malaysian border. The remaining 4.7 percent belong to several small groups, such as Vietnamese, Khmer, Mon, and several hill tribes of the north. In general, there is little friction among the ethnic groups.

Most people—80 percent or more—live in villages, and Thai culture has traditionally been based on village life. People who have migrated to the cities usually have roots in

Who Lives in Thailand?	
Thai	79.5%
Chinese	12.1%
Malay	3.7%
Khmer	2.7%
Other	2.0%

Village housing along the Ping River in Chiang Mai

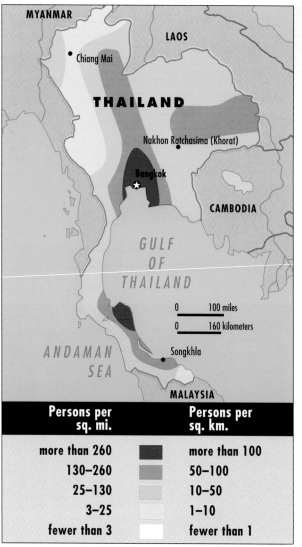

Populations of Thailand's Largest Cities (1991)

Bangkok	5,620,591
Nonthaburi	264,201
Nakhon Ratchasima	202,503
Chiang Mai	161,541
Khon Kaen	131,478

a village and return often to visit their relatives. During the boom years of the early 1990s, this began to change. Many people left the villages for work in cities—especially Bangkok.

The Southern Provinces

The people of the fourteen provinces along the narrow southern peninsula have a different lifestyle from people in other parts of Thailand. They have a southern accent, and many of them speak Malay as well as Thai. Many worship in Muslim mosques rather than Buddhist temples. The regional history also differs from that of the rest of the country. It was governed by local rulers and was not really a part of Thailand until the twentieth century.

People in the south are fishers, work on rubber or coconut plantations, or mine and process tin. A rapidly growing part

Language

Thai, also known as Siamese, is the official language of the nation. Different dialects are used in different parts of the country, but nearly everyone knows the official language. It is related to the Tai languages spoken in the neighboring countries of Myanmar, Laos, Vietnam, and parts of southern China. Some of the words have come directly from the Khmer, Pali, and Sanskrit languages.

Many Thais speak fluent English, which is a required subject in school from at least the fourth grade on. In some areas, the people also speak Malay or Chinese.

Thai is a tonal language. The meanings of words with a similar sound differ when spoken at different pitches—high, low, rising, and so forth. The written script consists of forty-four consonants and thirty-two vowel and diphthong symbols. The Thai alphabet was developed in 1283, during the Sukhothai period.

Language, oral and written, is a unifying element among Thai people. Grammar is simple, without any suffixes, genders, articles, or plurals. Thais love to laugh; slang and puns in the Thai language are popular and often outrageous.

The spelling of Thai words in the Roman alphabet varies from one source to another, since some sounds are not quite the same in the different languages. Here are a few common Thai words and expressions, spelled phonetically.

Hello, good morning, or good–bye	Sawatdi krap (by a male)
	Sawatdi kah (by a female)
How are you?	Sabai di ru?
I'm fine	Sabai di
Excuse me	Khothot
Thank you	Khopkhun
What is your name?	Khun chu arai?
Foreigner	Farang
Never mind, or It doesn't matter	Mai pen rai
Fun, joyousness	Sanuk

Names

All Thais have two legal names. The given name comes first, the family name second. Thais generally use first names in conversation, perhaps with a title, such as Khun (Mr., Mrs., or Miss). So, if your name is Peter, a Thai person may address you as Khun Peter.

Nearly every newborn Thai is given a nickname, as well as a "real" name. This nickname, a short, one-syllable word such as Ta, Ti, or Toon, sticks with a person for life. Many nicknames are the names of animals. Some, such as "rat" or "pig," would be considered rather insulting in English. Nicknames are used more often than either first or last names. When one Thai introduces another Thai to a foreigner, he may say, "This is Mr. Moo (Mr. Pig)."

of the economy in the south is based on tourism. The beaches and other natural attractions lure vacationers from the rest of Thailand and from other countries. Phuket Island is a popular destination.

Guides await tourists at the ever-popular Phangnga Bay.

The Hill Tribes

The 250,000 to 500,000 people who live in the far north of Thailand belong to ten or more tribal groups. Thais call them the *chao khao*, which means "mountain people." These people are seminomadic and have traditionally moved back and forth across the borders with neighboring countries without any particular national loyalty. In recent years, however, a number of them have been more assimilated into Thai life. As deforestation has changed the landscape in the north, some of the tribal people have moved down to the lowlands.

People of the various tribes have their own distinct lifestyles, religious beliefs, dialects, and, in many cases, clothing. The women, especially, wear elaborate and colorful handwoven and embroidered costumes. Many of them are skillful craftspeople.

Bicycles are a convenient way to travel the streets of Chiang Mai.

This region is in the so-called Golden Triangle, which includes parts of Thailand, Myanmar, and Laos. A major cash crop has traditionally been poppies, which were sold to opium dealers. While this industry made a lot of money for drug dealers, the farmers got very little of it. Thailand is administering several governmental and royal programs to bring education to the area. A major aim is widespread crop substitution. When successful, these programs will give farmers the opportunity to raise less harmful products and, at the same time, will help raise the standard of living among the hill tribes.

Chiang Mai is the major city of northern Thailand and the gateway to the mountain villages of the hill tribes. Tourists—both from other parts of Thailand and from other

countries—enjoy visiting Chiang Mai. They come to relax; the pace is pleasantly slower than in Bangkok. They also come for the breathtaking mountain scenery and the fascinating ancient temples. Shopping is another main attraction; many fine crafts, handmade by artisans of the region, are sold in Chiang Mai's street markets.

Opposite: **Women from the mountain villages go to small towns and cities to sell their beautiful, handwoven crafts.**

Women in Thailand

In many Western countries, women have risen to success and power in political life more than in the world of work. The opposite is true in Thailand. Rural Thai women traditionally played an important role in the rural economy. Family property was passed down through the females, and the family farm was often managed by the family matriarch (the female head

In the city, some Thai women have careers in hotels.

of the household). There was no philosophy that a woman's place was in the home!

Urban Chinese-Thais who worked in commerce also took women into the workforce. They worked as lawyers, accountants, and marketers, though men played the dominant roles. Today, women make up 70 percent of the Thai workforce. Young women leave farms for jobs in the city in order to contribute to the family income.

In 1990, more women than men graduated from institutions of higher learning. Thus, women are gaining more leading positions in business and the professions. In government, however, only a small number of posts are held by women, even at the village level.

Marriage

Young people in Thailand are free to choose their own marriage partners. The wedding ceremony is usually not elaborate nor especially religious. Traditionally, the marriage day begins with merit-making. Early in the morning, the couple presents food and small gifts to local monks and receives their blessing. A senior monk sprinkles water on the bride and groom and wedding guests.

Later, a loop of white thread is tied around the bride and groom's heads or wrists, and the two loops are linked together. This symbolizes the union of two individuals. Then the party begins. Family members and friends gather for food, drink, music, and dancing. The marriage is then recorded at the district office, which makes it legal.

In rural areas, it is customary for the groom to move in with the bride's family after the marriage and help out on the family farm.

Education

In Thailand about a hundred and fifty years ago, only aristocrats and monks were educated. Those who learned to read and write were taught in the wats. The reign of King Mongkut was a turning point. He valued education and hired a teacher to teach his children English and Latin. His successor, King Chulalongkorn, opened a school in the palace, then other schools outside. He established a Department of Education to set up primary schools throughout the kingdom.

Chiang Mai University

In 1932, a law called for four years of public school for all children. Some remote parts of the country had no schools, but by 1990, more than 95 percent of young people between seven and twelve years old were in classes. Schools are expected to provide lunches and health-care services. Recently, compulsory education was increased to six years. The government plans to make public education through high school available to all.

There are twenty state universities in Thailand, including twelve in Bangkok. There are also twenty-six private colleges and universities.

The Unifying Faith

At least 95 percent of the people in Thailand are Buddhists. Buddhism is a powerful force that unites the Thai people, along with love of their country and their king.

Buddhism started in India more than two thousand years ago. Over several centuries, its followers spread their beliefs throughout eastern Asia. Today, Buddhism is the major faith in Myanmar, Thailand, Laos, Cambodia, Tibet, Korea, Japan, and Mongolia, as well as in Thailand.

According to Buddhist teachings, a young prince lived in India nearly 600 years before the birth of Christ. His ideas about the meaning of life and how people should live became one of the world's great religions. His name was Siddhārtha Gautama. He is remembered as the Buddha, the Enlightened One.

The Buddha's teachings were based on Four Noble Truths: (1) life is suffering, (2) suffering comes from cravings or desires, (3) suffering can cease, (4) there is a way people can stop suffering. The way to end suffering, according to the Buddha, is to follow the Eightfold Path. Once a person has learned right understanding, right thought, right speech, right conduct, right livelihood, right effort, right attentiveness, and right concentration, he or she will achieve enlightenment and will no longer suffer.

Different Buddhist sects have developed in different parts of the world. Most Thais are Theravada Buddhists.

Opposite: **The interior of the Wat Koo Tao Temple in Chiang Mai**

Buddhism and Everyday Life

Buddhism is a faith, a system of morality and ethics, and a philosophy of life. It teaches kindness and tolerance toward everyone, regardless of race, creed, or nationality. It also teaches that everything a person does has an effect. Selfishness results in unhappiness; kind and unselfish acts bring happiness. What a person is and what happens to him or her is one's *karma*, the result of one's own actions.

Buddhists also believe in reincarnation—that a person has other lives before and after this one. The kind of next life one has also depends on one's actions in this life. Therefore, it is important to do good deeds, to "make merit." Giving food to monks, building and renovating monasteries and hospitals, and doing kind deeds in general, are ways of making merit.

Buddhists bow in the traditional wai position as they bring offerings to the Buddha.

Buddhist Monks

People visiting Thailand for the first time are surprised at how many men they see everywhere dressed in orange-yellow, or saffron, robes draped over one shoulder. Their heads are shaved, and they are barefoot or wear simple thong sandals. These are Buddhist monks.

One reason why there are so many of them is that nearly every Buddhist male—even the king—spends one or more

Opposite: **Young monks**

Some students of Buddhism attend school at the Wat Po Temple in Bangkok.

periods of his life as a monk. This may be done at any stage of life, from boyhood to a man's last years. It may be for a very short time or as long as one pleases. A monk is free to return to secular life at any time. Many government agencies and some large companies grant a male employee a four-month leave of absence, with pay, to enter the monkhood temporarily.

Monks live in monasteries and spend much time there in meditation. They eat only donated food, which they collect from households each morning. There are 227 rules of conduct to be followed. At the same time, freedom of thought is encouraged. Questions and lively discussions about Buddha's teachings are common.

For three months during the rainy season, monks remain in the monasteries overnight and concentrate on their religious duties. This period, the Buddhist Lent, is also the time when young men entering

Visakha Puja

Visakha Puja is a religious holiday that celebrates the birth, enlightenment, and death of the Buddha. Based on the lunar calendar, the holiday usually falls in May. During the day, ceremonies and sermons are held in the temples. In the evening, everyone joins in torch-light walks to the chapel carrying flowers, a lighted candle, and three burning incense sticks.

their temporary monkhood are usually ordained. These are important occasions in village life. The novice hosts a party for friends the night before the ordination. In the morning, the novice, with his head shaved and dressed in a white robe, parades to the monastery with dancing and drumbeats, along with the elder monks and the people of the village. Then they walk clockwise three times around the chapel. After ordination, he changes his white robes for saffron ones.

Some Thai women choose to live a monastic life as nuns. They shave their heads, take vows, and spend their time in study and meditation, just as the monks do. However, they are not given as much respect and attention by the general public as monks are, nor are they officially equal to them.

Wats

Nearly every village in Thailand has a wat. There are 28,000 of them in Thailand. Typically, a wat is a tree-shaded, walled Buddhist compound with several buildings. Traditional Thai architecture features multiple steep and sharply pointed roof levels with richly decorated gables. There are three important types of religious buildings: A *bot* houses important images of Buddha and is used for such ceremonies as ordinations of monks. A *viharn*

A typical
Thai temple

The Temple of the Emerald Buddha

When Rama I decided to establish his capital at Bangkok, his first project was to build a Royal Chapel to house the Emerald Buddha. This chapel, Wat Phra Keo, adjoins the Grand Palace and is used by the king for special ceremonies and celebrations. Within the chapel is a small but dazzling 600-year-old statue, the most famous and venerated religious image in Thailand. Made of a type of jade, the figure is 30 inches (75 cm) high and sits on top of a 36-foot (11-m) golden altar. Tourists come to marvel at the splendid art objects surrounding the statue. Devoted Buddhists come to worship, bearing offerings of fragrant flowers and *joss* (incense) sticks.

At the beginning of each of Thailand's three seasons (hot, rainy, and cool), the king comes to the Temple of the Emerald Buddha to preside over a ceremony. He changes the robes draped over the Buddha figure. There is a golden tunic, decorated with diamonds, for the hot season. The one for the rainy season is gilded, with flecks of blue. For the cool season, the figure is dressed in an enamel-coated solid-gold robe.

also has images of Buddha, but it is a simpler building, used for meditation and meetings. A *stupa,* a building topped with a spire, is a shrine. One type of stupa is called a *chedi.* Several other buildings are within the compound, including living quarters for the monks.

The primary purpose of a wat is religious, but in many villages it is used for many other purposes, too. It may include a school, clinic, or hostel and sometimes an orphanage and home for the aged or mentally ill. It serves as an information, employment, and recreation center.

Buddhist monks conducting a funeral

Funeral ceremonies are held on the grounds of the wat. Three days after a person dies, a funeral procession accompanies the coffin to the village wat. The monks, family members, and villagers pour water over the body as a blessing. Then the corpse is cremated.

Monks are community leaders and they provide a variety of important services. They counsel people in trouble, listen to disputes, and arbitrate conflicts. They were the principal educators for centuries. Before government schools were established, the only schools for children were in wats. In some small and remote villages, this is still true.

The Hindu Heritage

Prince Siddhārtha Gautama, the Buddha, was born and brought up in the Hindu tradition. Hinduism had already spread over much of southern and Southeast Asia when Buddhism was introduced. The Buddha never claimed to be a god, and Buddhist followers did not try to wipe out earlier beliefs. For this reason, many Hindu deities and symbols are used in Buddhist art and architecture.

A stone statue at Wat Khaek in Nong Khai

Figures of the three main Hindu deities—Vishnu, Shiva, and Brahma—are often seen. The four-armed Vishnu is the Protector. He sometimes takes other forms and names, such as Rama and Krishna. Shiva is the Destroyer, sometimes pictured as a ten-armed god dancing the universe to destruction. Brahma is the Creator.

Other lesser gods and creatures frequently encountered are Ganesha, Shiva's elephant-headed son; Garuda, the half-bird, half-man creature who carried Vishnu wherever he traveled; and numerous *nagas*, many-headed serpents who came from the underworld.

Flowers decorate a Buddhist spirit house.

Animism

Animism, a belief that good and bad spirits control natural forces, is even older and more widespread than Hinduism in many parts of Asia. Just about every Thai home and public building—even most wats—has a spirit house outside. Recognition of these spirits, like the Hindu gods, is simply incorporated into the practice of Buddhism.

A spirit house is a miniature Thai house set on a pedestal. Spirit houses guarding public buildings are much larger and more elaborate, almost like temples. They are built as residences

Opposite: **Muslim boys**

**Religions of
Thailand**

Buddhist	94.8%
Muslim	4.0%
Christian	0.6%
Other	0.6%

**Young Muslim women at
a religious school**

for the spirits, to keep them out of mischief. Offerings of fresh fruits and flowers are placed in the spirit houses daily, to keep the spirits happy.

Other Religions

Muslims, those who practice the religion of Islam, are the largest religious minority in Thailand, but they make up only about 4 percent of the total population. Almost all of them live in the four southernmost provinces, in the Malay Peninsula. Many are of Malay descent.

Islam is supported by the king, in his capacity as upholder of all religions. He presides over certain Muslim celebrations. The government provides funds to build Muslim mosques and schools. There are about two thousand mosques in Thailand and some two hundred Muslim schools.

A devout Muslim is expected to make a pilgrimage to the holy city of Mecca, a *hajj*, once in his life. Just as some Thai

men are given paid leaves of absence of four months to serve as temporary monks, some Muslims are granted a similar privilege to make a hajj.

Only about 0.6 percent of the population of Thailand are Christians. Another 0.6 percent are mostly Indian Hindus and Sikhs.

Leisure Time

Half a dozen young men and women are seated on a scaffolding high above the floor of a temple. With tiny brushes and dishes of paint, they are adding details to a huge mural. Not far away in the same wat, a few older men are carving a wooden statue. Other artisans are engraving patterns on sheets of gold and silver.

Thai artists build unusual creations to adorn their buildings.

Opposite: **Elaborately painted lacquer doors greet visitors at the Temple of the Great Relic in Bangkok.**

THESE CRAFTSPEOPLE ARE WORKing on a restoration project in one of Thailand's thousands of wats. The time is now. But the scene might have been Sukhothai 750 years ago. Or Ayutthaya a century after that. Or Bangkok at the end of the eighteenth century. Artists have been creating and preserving works of beauty in temples and palaces in Thailand for more years than one can count. Various skills have been handed down within a family or village, from generation to generation.

The government of Thailand is restoring many of the nation's ancient treasures, so that they can be open to visitors. The early capitals of Sukhothai and Ayutthaya are now historical parks, designated World Heritage Sites by the United Nations. Many sculptures and artifacts are on display either in their original settings or in the park museums.

The National Museum

The buildings that house Bangkok's National Museum are as old as the city itself. They once included a home for the "second king," a position like that of a vice president, but that office no longer exists. A large collection of prehistoric art is displayed in the former palace.

This museum is the largest in Southeast Asia and contains Buddhist art from almost every Asian country. The Thai collection covers all periods up to the present. One interesting display features traditional musical instruments from Laos, Cambodia, and Indonesia as well as from Thailand. Another exhibit has pieces of furniture used by early kings and their families.

The Buddhaisawan Chapel, which was the second king's private place of worship, has a much-prized bronze sculpture of the Buddha and some outstanding murals depicting his life.

Classical Arts

The early rulers were patrons of the arts who encouraged and sponsored architects and artists to build and decorate these great structures. Certain forms were followed—artists were not expected to come up with unusual creations. Nearly all classical artistic works were related to religion.

Since Buddhism came to Thailand from India, the religious arts were greatly influenced by the traditions of India and Hinduism. Brilliant colors, many different materials, and intricate details are characteristics of Thai arts and crafts.

Bangkok is crowded with modern skyscrapers and sacred temples and mosques.

Architecture

Architecture is the most visible and the most social of all art forms. People can choose whether or not to look at paintings or sculpture, whether or not to listen to music or watch a dramatic performance. But architecture surrounds us. We cannot avoid seeing buildings and being influenced in some way by their shapes and styles and colors.

The Grand Palace

The first task undertaken by Rama I when he became king of Thailand was to start construction of the Grand Palace (right), a large, walled compound in the heart of Bangkok. It is the most important spot in the nation and the most visited, both by the Thai people and by foreign visitors.

The walls surrounding the structures are nearly 6,300 feet (1,920 m) long. A double gate leads to the front court. To the left are three main buildings—an audience hall where various ceremonies are held, another hall used for coronations, and the residence of the first three Chakri kings.

A throne is in the front of the audience hall, backed by a boat-shaped altar. A canopy over the throne is made of nine tiers of white cloth. The coronation chair, an octagonal seat, and an altar are the focus of attention in the next hall. While kings have not lived in the residence for many years, it is customary for a newly crowned sovereign to spend one night there. In this way, the historic building is still recognized as a royal residence.

A second group of buildings is called the Dusit group. The walls are white with many levels of steep green and red roofs pointing upward. Lightning-shaped finials (ornaments) rise from each point and level of the roofs. In an audience hall in this group, a throne covered with mother-of-pearl is topped by another nine-tiered canopy.

The Chakri group of buildings was built by King Chulalongkorn (Rama V), who reigned at the turn of the twentieth century. A reception hall is used to greet foreign dignitaries and representatives to Thailand. Four paintings on the walls depict historic diplomatic receptions, and many of the crystal decorations in this hall were

gifts to King Chulalongkorn from foreign monarchs.

The Boromabiman building was the royal residence for the next four kings. Rama VI was responsible for a group of frescoes illustrating the Vedic gods of India. The Ten Kingly Virtues are written beneath the gods: giving, right conduct, personal sacrifice, honesty, humility, concentration, freedom from anger, freedom from malice, patience, and avoidance of wrongdoing.

A connecting gate leads from the royal residence to the grounds of the Royal Chapel of the Emerald Buddha

(opposite, below). These grounds contain all the elements of a monastery except a residential quarter. Monks do not live here.

About two dozen other buildings and monuments stand within the Grand Palace compound. Several contain images of the Buddha and murals depicting his life. Statues of mythological animals and of elephants stand outside. Galleries surrounding the grounds are decorated with murals that tell the story of the *Ramakian,* the Thai version of the Indian epic *Ramayana.*

A wall painting at Wat Phra Keo in Bangkok

While Thailand's architecture—especially in its religious structures—shows some influences of older civilizations and surrounding countries, it is also unique. The towers and spires and upwardly pointing roofs come in many materials and colors, but they are all quite recognizable as Thai architecture. Older private dwellings are equally distinctive, with steep roofs and decorative touches.

Modern Thai cities are crowded with tall skyscrapers made of glass, steel, and concrete—just like those in Toronto or Dallas or Hong Kong. But mixed in with these tall, boxlike structures are the exotic shapes and colors of temples and shrines. Slim spire-topped cones covered with gold or shiny tiles dazzle the eye, and green and orange roofs with jagged ornaments jut upward at each gable. The buildings are decorated with marble platforms, bronze lions, and inlaid doors. Almost every surface is covered with glass mosaic, mother-of-pearl, gold leaf, paint, lacquer, silk fabric, or bits of porcelain.

Painting

Early murals and book illustrations depicted stories from Hindu and Buddhist literature, painted against beautiful landscapes. Scenes of everyday life in Thailand were sometimes used. The colors in older paintings were subdued, because of the kind of pigments that were available. More recent ones used bolder paints imported from China and from Western sources. The use of gold leaf brightened the pictures even more.

Contemporary Thai painters have been trained in the traditional styles and techniques but have added modern, individualistic touches. One of the best-known painters is Chakrapan Posayakrit, whose works include portraits and literary scenes and characters.

Sculpture

Early Thai sculpture was confined almost exclusively to stylized figures of the Buddha and the Hindu gods and spirits. Buddha figures were made of smooth, sleek materials such as highly polished stone, wood, or metal. To emphasize the serenity and meditative aspect of Buddhism, the

Silpa Bhirasri

In 1924, an Italian sculptor named Corado Feroci arrived in Thailand to work with the Royal Fine Arts Department. This move changed both the artist's life and the future of art in Thailand.

Feroci founded a school of fine arts, which became Silpakorn University in 1943. The following year he became a Thai citizen and changed his name to Silpa Bhirasri. He served on the faculty of the university until his death. Many of his students have achieved fame both in Thailand and abroad. Silpa is considered to be the father of modern art in Thailand.

A serene Buddha smiles upon the world at Wat Chedi Luang in Chiang Mai.

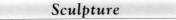

figures are symbolic rather than realistic. No distracting wrinkles or other lifelike details were included.

Modern sculptors have created realistic statues of kings and other historic figures. One well-known Thai artist is Misiem Yipintsoi. Some of her works are on display in a sculpture garden she established in Bajhon Pathom, near Bangkok.

Creating lacquerware is a fine art.

Other Arts and Crafts

Lacquerware is made by artisans in the province of Chiang Mai. The process starts with a frame made of wood, such as bamboo, which has been formed into the shape of a bowl, plate, tray, or other object. Workers apply a mixture made of local natural materials. Several coats of this mixture, then several coats of a pure black lacquer, are applied in this way. Each coat is allowed to dry, then the worker polishes the piece before applying the next coat. Finally, a colored pattern is applied over the shiny black surface. Some pieces are decorated with gold leaf, while others are inlaid with tiny pieces of mother-of-pearl.

The shaping and firing of fine pottery may be the oldest art form in this part of the world. Some pots found in archaeological digs were made as far back as 5,000 years ago. Celadon pottery, a delicate blue-green color, was introduced to

Jim Thompson, a Mystery

Jim Thompson, an American who lived in Bangkok for twenty years after World War II (1939–1945), is remembered fondly for his help in promoting the Thai silk industry. He founded a company that sold silk to European fashion leaders. Thai silk became popular around the world at a time when the industry was in danger of dying out.

Thompson was passionately fond of the traditional arts of Southeast Asia. His home in Bangkok was made by attaching several Thai-style houses together and surrounding them with a beautiful garden. He then filled the rooms with Chinese porcelains, Burmese wood carvings, and Cambodian and Thai stone sculptures. His house is now a museum, open to visitors.

Jim Thompson's death is an unsolved mystery. While on vacation in Malaysia, he went out for a walk and was never seen again.

artists in the Sukhothai kingdom by Chinese potters. Pottery soon became an important product in trading with other regions, and the art has recently been revived in the north of Thailand.

Thai silk, prized around the world, is the most famous of all Thai handicrafts. Women in the villages of northeast Thailand tend the mulberry trees, raise silkworms (which feed on mulberry leaves), spin and dye silk thread, and weave bolts of brilliant, shimmering, silk cloth. The beautiful fabrics in patterns and solid colors are sold all over the world. Dressmakers and tailors in Thai cities create fashionable custom-made garments for men and women. Many tourists in Thailand buy some Thai silk to take home.

Thai cotton is increasingly popular, too. In the northern hill country, villagers embroider designs on strips of homespun cotton and hemp. The strips are made into shoulder bags and other brightly colored objects. The hand-painted cotton umbrellas made in northern Thailand are attractive souvenirs and great protection from Thailand's intense sunlight.

Silkworms growing in baskets

Thai silk is admired worldwide.

The intricate work of Thai silversmiths is famous.

Ornamental silverwork from Thailand is also famous. Artisans cut and shape thin sheets of silver into bowls, boxes, jewelry, and other attractive objects. For some pieces, they punch many tiny holes to create a filigree.

Another silver craft is nielloware, a system of engraving and treating a piece to create an embossed, or raised, effect. Tea sets, desk sets, and many other beautiful art pieces are made of pure silver, sometimes gold-plated.

SUPPORT

Thai crafts were traditionally done in people's homes where parents taught their skills to their children. Some crafts have become less popular in recent years, and Queen Sirikit has worked to encourage people to preserve them. She established SUPPORT (The Foundation for the Promotion of Supplementary Occupations and Related Techniques) to provide training to farmers and their families. The sale of top-quality crafts provides extra income for rural communities.

Performing Arts

Music has been an important part of life in Thailand since ancient times. During the Ayutthaya period, musical instruments from India and the Khmer and Mon cultures came into the kingdom. Soon, uniquely Thai instruments were invented and used along with the imported ones.

About fifty types of Thai instruments, including variations of flutes, stringed instruments, and gongs, are used at festivals, weddings, funerals, and social gatherings. Princess Maha Chakri Sirindhorn has been a leader in the revival of traditional Thai music. She is also a noted performer on several Thai instruments.

Students practice their traditional musical instruments at the School for Dramatic Arts in Bangkok.

Classical Western music was brought into the country about a century ago. A number of Thai musicians have learned to play Western instruments, and in 1982, the Bangkok Symphony Orchestra was established.

Popular Western music and instruments have been well known in Thailand since the 1950s. Many young Thais enjoy playing the guitar. King Bhumibol is internationally recognized as a fine jazz musician and composer.

A masked drama enacting stories from the *Ramakian*

Several other traditional dance dramas are popular in Thailand. The *khon* is a masked drama and dance based on the *Ramakian*. The narrative is told by a chorus, accompanied by a musical group. The masks and costumes are elaborately decorated. Shadow plays and marionette shows are not often performed today, but puppets are made and sold in craft markets.

Literature

The kings of Thailand have been authors since the early kingdom of Sukhothai. Rama I, who founded the Chakri Dynasty, worked with a group of scholars to put together the *Ramakian*. His work is also a record of medieval court customs.

Phya Anuman Rajadhon, who lived from 1888 to 1969, wrote many books about Thai culture and folklore. Several distinguished Thai novelists of this century are known by their pen names, including Dokmaisod, Mae Anong, Kan Phungbun Na Ayudhya, and Sri Burapha.

Sports

Sports are part of school programs in Thailand. Most children participate in activities such as table tennis, gymnastics, basketball, volleyball, and track and field. Soccer is probably the most popular sport in the nation. Young people play it in school, and people of all ages follow the game as a spectator sport. Televised matches attract millions of enthusiastic viewers. Thailand is a participant in the international Asian Games, and Thai athletes have won many medals.

Bangkok has several sports clubs. Facilities include racetracks, swimming pools, gyms, tennis courts, playing fields, and golf courses. Thais are proud of the internationally famous golf champion Tiger Woods, whose mother is Thai. Sailing and yachting are also popular.

Tiger Woods

A demonstration of kickboxing

Some sports enjoyed in Thailand are not familiar in much of the world. For example, boxing has different rules in Thailand than in most other countries. To Westerners, it seems very violent. Boxers are allowed to use their feet, elbows, knees, and shoulders to kick or punch their opponents. However, biting, spitting, and wrestling are forbidden, and boxers must wear gloves.

Bullfighting in Thailand is different, too. The bulls fight each other, and the spectators bet on their favorites. An elephant festival in Thailand features a rodeo. One event is a tug-of-war between an elephant and a hundred or so men. Another act is an elephant race.

Kite-flying is popular during the windy season. During March and April, whenever the winds are right, the air is full of huge kites over the Pramane Grounds near the Royal Palace in Bangkok. As a competitive sport, two teams try to force one anothers' kites to fall to the ground.

Everyday Life

From the days of the Sukhothai kingdom to the space age, Thailand's prosperity came from the land. Products of the rice fields and forests were plentiful enough to meet the nation's needs and provide surpluses for use in international trade.

After the family, the village was the center of everyday life. Almost everyone either lived in rural areas or had close family ties there. People expected to spend their entire lives in the village where they and their ancestors were born.

Life began to change for many Thais in the 1980s. Industry in Thailand expanded with lightning speed. Suddenly, rice was no longer the main export; it had fallen to tenth place. Jobs in the cities lured young people away from farms and villages. The huge difference between the cities and villages began to diminish. Better transportation made travel to and from urban areas easier and faster. Television and movies brought the outside world into regions that had once been remote.

Children in the Village

A Thai family is usually made up of several generations. Grandparents live either with the younger people or in a separate house nearby. In many ways, a Thai village functions as an even more extended family. The monastery, the school, and the village government hold the villagers together. Decisions are made by consensus, rather than by a small group of leaders. Social, religious, and community life are all intertwined.

Children are protected, even pampered. Before school age they are rarely, if ever, scolded. They are also given a lot of freedom. They can come and go pretty much as they please to play with other village children. All the adults feel a responsibility to see that children are safe and cared for whether or not they are related to them.

Village families don't have a lot of money to spend on store-bought toys. Many children and their parents make toys out of the natural materials at hand—such as leaves, bits of wood, and clay.

Life is simple for many Thai villagers.

Education—six years of school—is required of all children. They start at age five or six. Their parents feel strongly about education and make sure children keep up with their studies.

At about the same age, most rural children begin to help out with family chores. Farmers' children feed the chickens and other animals, lead livestock out to the fields, baby-sit their younger sisters and brothers, and help in the rice fields. Many Thai children learn to swim well at an early age. Fish are hatching in the rice paddies during the wet season, and young children swim out with nets and baskets to catch them.

If the family has a business, children begin to learn about it at an early age. They start to weave, make baskets, paint decorations on pottery, or help sell produce at a market. By the time they are teenagers, they have a skill, and their contributions to the family income are quite important. As they grow older, they take part in family discussions and help make decisions about both business and personal matters.

Opposite: **A family fishes in the Mekong Delta.**

Holidays in Thailand

New Year's Day	January 1
Makha Puja	February
Chakri Day	April 6
Songkran	April 13
Labor Day	May
Coronation Day	May 5
Visakha Puja	May
Asanha Puja	July
Queen's Birthday	August 12
Loi Krathong	Late October/ Early November
King's Birthday	December 5
Constitution Day	December 10

Village Social Life

Village homes are simple, often made of wood by members of the family. Many houses are set up on stilts, with space underneath to shelter livestock and protect people and possessions from flash floods. Houses are thought of as places to sleep, not to entertain friends.

A typical Thai house built on stilts

The entire community celebrates important occasions together—ordinations, funerals, marriages, and festivals. Farmers cooperate with one another for the big jobs of planting and irrigating; workers construct houses or public buildings together. Village women gather together before religious holidays to prepare food for the monks.

A Thai girl makes a toy for her younger sister.

Villagers treat outsiders who come to visit with friendliness and consideration. Thai children are taught to avoid conflict and that politeness is very important. Displays of anger are considered to be signs of ignorance and immaturity.

Respect for elders is a deeply honored element of the Buddhist way of life. Younger siblings look up to older brothers and sisters; parents to grandparents. Parents and grandparents are never neglected as they grow older and less active. Younger people take for granted a responsibility to care for older family members.

This respect for elders and people in authority carries over into adult life and the outside world. Thai students rarely question the opinions of their teachers. Even in business and government, young men and women are reluctant to oppose anything suggested by their seniors.

Festivals

Two annual festivals are celebrated with great gusto all over Thailand. These are Songkran and Loi Krathong. The king's and queen's birthdays are honored, as are various Buddhist holidays and regional fairs and festivals.

People throwing water to celebrate Songkran

Songkran is the celebration of the New Year, according to the Thai lunar calendar. It usually falls in April. People who have moved from villages to cities come home to enjoy this holiday with their families. In some regions, the partying goes on for days.

Celebration of Songkran involves a thorough housecleaning; presentation of gifts to monks, elders, and spirits; pilgrimages to holy shrines; releasing of caged birds; parades and dances; and general merrymaking.

Songkran comes during the hot, dry season, shortly before the big rains. People anticipate the rains by splashing a lot of water on one another. Anyone on the street is apt to get an unexpected dousing from a friend—or a complete stranger. Soon after Songkran, it is time to plant a new rice crop. Chiang Mai is a favorite place to celebrate Songkran. There are parades, religious ceremonies, beauty contests, and lots of water throwing.

A daytime parade in celebration of Loi Krathong

An annual Elephant Roundup is held in mid-November at the Surin Sports Stadium in northeast Thailand. More than a hundred elephants demonstrate amazing skills. An Elephant Village and Study Center is being developed to help preserve these wonderful animals. Several major Thai corporations are helping support the center.

The most beautiful festival of all in Thailand is celebrated in late October or November. Loi Krathong is held on a night when the moon is full. A traditional *krathong* is a tiny basket, or boat, made of woven banana leaves. People place flowers, incense, candles, and coins on krathongs and set them afloat on a river. The candlelight twinkles for miles and miles on the water—a lovely light to see.

Television and Movies

Communication has had a great deal to do with changing lifestyles in Thailand. More than 80 percent of Thai homes had television sets by 1995. The nation has several television channels, including some cable broadcasts, and nearly five hundred radio stations. Serial dramas, sports programs, quiz and game shows, and talk shows are popular. Nearly all are produced in Thailand.

As in Western countries, television commercials advertise all kinds of products and use glamorous stars to promote them. And even though more TV viewers live in rural areas, usually an urban way of life is depicted.

Thai television also airs university-level educational programs. They reach an enthusiastic audience of students working toward an academic degree.

Thai movie producers turn out popular entertainment films. In addition, many imported movies, mostly from the United States, play to good-size audiences.

Clothing

Multiple television screens in a shopping mall

Villagers in Thailand wear simple clothing, appropriate to the hot climate. For men, shorts and shirts are common. They also often wear a checkered rectangle of cotton cloth loosely tied around the waist, which can serve as a turban, bandana, towel, or loincloth. Women usually wear wraparound skirts and a blouse.

In both the cities and the villages, formal dress-up clothing is usually just about the same as in most Western cities.

Food

Thai food was relatively unknown in the United States and Canada a generation ago. Today, however, many Thai restaurants are found in major cities of North America. In addition, some restaurants feature a variety of dishes from several Asian countries, and chefs like to use spices and herbs popular in Asia to create a new international cuisine. Chilies, curries, lemongrass, onions, ginger, garlic, and mint are among the more popular elements used to add flavor to meat, seafood, and vegetables. Dipping sauces accompany many different dishes. Rice is nearly always served as a side dish.

Pad Thai is often found on the menu in a Thai restaurant. That name is sort of a general name, though, and the ingredients vary from one kitchen to another. Every cook has his or her own version. It's a stir-fried noodle dish, with bits of meat, seafood, and vegetables, flavored with fish sauce, soy sauce, chilies, and spices. Chopped peanuts may be added as a garnish.

There are no food taboos in Thai Buddhism. A farang might be startled to see northeastern Thais eating fried ants or grasshoppers. Seafood is a staple in southern Thailand, but some of it is quite unusual elsewhere, such as jellyfish salad.

Tropical fruits—mangoes, papayas, jackfruit, and others—are plentiful and delicious. Sweetened coconut milk is used to make many desserts.

Great pains are taken to make the food a delight to the eye as well as to the taste buds. Tiny tomatoes are carved into roses, watermelons are shaped into vases, and decorative fish are formed from cucumbers. Ice cream or custard may be served in a small coconut half, and cookies may be presented in a basket woven of banana leaves.

In the words of one Thai gentleman, "We always cook plenty. We want to have enough left over to feed the dogs and give to the monks next morning."

A Teenager in Bangkok

Fon is a thirteen-year-old girl living in Bangkok. Her parents grew up in a village, but Fon has always lived in the city. Each morning she gets dressed in her school uniform, a white blouse and dark red skirt. She likes school and gets good grades, especially in math and science. "I want to be a doctor or a science teacher when I grow up," Fon says.

After school, she does her homework each day; then she likes to ride her bike, watch television, or go to a mall. "I like to look at fashion magazines and window-shop, because I get bored with that same old skirt!"

Most of Fon's leisure time is spent with her family. She enjoys cooking with her mother, and she's proud of the delicious meals she can make. On weekends and holidays, she and her family usually drive out of town. They visit her grandparents in the country or go to a national park or the beach. "Last month we visited some of the Khmer ruins in the northeast, and soon we want to spend a weekend in Chiang Mai," she says.

Fon plans to get a degree from a Thai university. "Then I'd like to visit North America. Maybe I'll go to graduate school there, but I'll always be glad to come back to Thailand. I wouldn't want to live anywhere else."

However, Thai women are fond of a distinctive Thai-style suit that consists of a long-sleeved, high-necked jacket buttoned down the front and a slim, long skirt. Thai-made silk and cotton fabrics come in many lovely colors and prints.

Bangkok Today

Bangkok is Thailand's largest city. One of every ten Thais lives there. It is forty-five times the size of Chiang Mai, the next largest city. It has long been the governmental, cultural, and educational center of the nation. Today, many of the urban values and customs are changing the lifestyle in villages.

Many people in Bangkok live in apartment buildings called shop houses. These are tall buildings with stores or

Modern, middle-class families in Bangkok live differently from families in rural villages.

other businesses on the first floor and apartments for owners and employees in the upper stories.

In contrast to village life, where the culture has been shaped largely by tradition and older people, Bangkok is a young people's city. Whether they are natives of Bangkok or came here from the country, young adults are adopting new fashions, customs, and ways of living. Popular songs have Thai lyrics played to music borrowed from Western rock. The words deal with romance and often with problems of living in the city. Concerts draw large audiences.

While people still believe in Buddhist values, many of the practices are changing. No longer is the wat the center of community activities. Many people go to a wat only for special religious ceremonies. People who would have visited the village wat every morning and evening for meditation now do most of their meditating in front of one or more Buddha images at the family altar at home.

Young married couples in Bangkok often set up housekeeping independently instead of moving in with their elders. Both husband and wife often have to work to support themselves, whether or not there are children. But their jobs will not usually be in the same place or doing the same type of work. This is quite different from village life, where the whole family usually works together in related activities.

Bangkok is big, crowded, polluted, noisy, and fast paced. But to young Thai people, it is exciting to be where the action is. They are happy to live in the city but eager to leave it for weekends and holidays in the country.

The twenty-first century will bring great changes all over the world, especially to developing countries such as Thailand. This nation will inevitably become less rural, less village-centered, less dependent on agriculture, and more involved in international affairs. But, whatever happens, the social values and traditions of this fascinating country are bound to endure.

A century from now, may Thailand still be known as the Land of Smiles.

Opposite: **Students outside Bangkok University**

Thai traditions will survive future changes to the nation.

Timeline

World History

c. 2500 B.C.   Egyptians build the Pyramids and Sphinx in Giza.

563 B.C.   Buddha is born in India.

A.D. 313   The Roman emperor Constantine recognizes Christianity.

610   The prophet Muhammad begins preaching a new religion called Islam.

1054   The Eastern (Orthodox) and Western (Roman) Churches break apart.

1066   William the Conqueror defeats the English in the Battle of Hastings.

1095   Pope Urban II proclaims the First Crusade.

1215   King John seals the Magna Carta.

1300s   The Renaissance begins in Italy.

1347   The Black Death sweeps through Europe.

1453   Ottoman Turks capture Constantinople, conquering the Byzantine Empire.

1492   Columbus arrives in North America.

1500s   The Reformation leads to the birth of Protestantism.

1776   The Declaration of Independence is signed.

1789   The French Revolution begins.

Thailand History

1238 A.D.   Si Inthtrahit establishes a kingdom and capital city (both named Sukhothai).

1350   Ayutthaya takes control of Sukhothai

1569–1590   The Burmese take control of Ayutthaya and rule the kingdom.

1767   The Burmese invade Ayutthaya and destroy the city.

1782   King Taksin is deposed and executed. The Chakri Dynasty is founded by Chao Phraya Chakri.

	Thailand History		World History	
Isarasuntorn becomes Rama II.	1809			
Chetsadabodin is crowned Rama III.	1824			
Mongkut becomes Rama IV.	1851			
Chulalongkorn succeeds his father as Rama V.	1868		1865	The American Civil War ends.
Rama V surrenders Siamese territory in Indochina to France.	1893			
Additional Siamese territory is ceded to France.	1904			
The Malay states are ceded to Great Britain.	1907			
Vajiravudh become Rama VI.	1910		1914	World War I breaks out.
Prajadhipok is crowned Rama VII.	1925		1917	The Bolshevik Revolution brings Communism to Russia.
A group of civil servants and army officers seizes control of the government.	1932		1929	Worldwide economic depression begins.
Rama VII abdicates the throne. Prince Ananda Mahidol is chosen to be the next king.	1935			
A Council of Regents rules for Prince Ananda Mahidol.	1935 – 1945		1939	World War II begins, following the German invasion of Poland.
Phibun Songkhram, a military officer, leads the Thai government.	1938 – 1945			
Ananda Mahidol is crowned Rama VIII. Bhumibol Adulyadej is declared king of Thailand.	1946			
Bhumibol Adulyadej is crowned Rama IX.	1950		1957	The Vietnam War starts.
			1989	The Berlin Wall is torn down as Communism crumbles in Eastern Europe.
Thailand celebrates the Golden Jubilee Year of Rama IX's reign.	1996		1996	Bill Clinton is reelected U.S. president.

Fast Facts

Official name: Pratet Thai (Kingdom of Thailand)

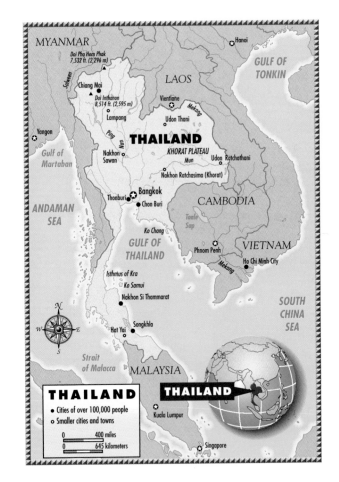

THAILAND
- • Cities of over 100,000 people
- ○ Smaller cities and towns

0   400 miles
0   645 kilometers

Capital: Bangkok

Official language: Thai

Flag of Thailand

Kao Sok National Park

Official religion:	Buddhism
National anthem:	Music by Phra Jenduriyang and words by Luang Saranuprabhandi
Government:	Constitutional monarchy with two legislative houses
Chief of state:	King
Head of government:	Prime minister
Area:	198,115 sq. mi. (513,115 sq km)
Coordinates of geographic center:	15° N 100° E
Bordering countries:	Thailand is bordered on the north and west by Myanmar, on the northeast by Laos, on the southeast by Cambodia and the Gulf of Thailand, on the south by Malaysia, and on the southwest by the Andaman Sea and Myanmar.
Highest elevation:	Doi Inthanon, 8,514 feet (2,595 m)
Lowest elevation:	Sea level

Average temperatures:

	April	December
Bangkok:	86°F (30°C)	77°F (25°C)

Average annual rainfall:

In the north, west, and central regions	60 inches (152 cm)
On the Khorat Plateau	50 inches (127 cm)

National population (1996): 60,003,000

Population of largest cities in Thailand (1991):

Bangkok	5,620,591
Nonthaburi	264,201
Nakhon Ratchasima	202,503
Chiang Mai	161,541
Khon Kaen	131,478

Famous landmarks:

▶ *Ayutthaya.* The Thai capital from 1350 to 1767, contains extensive ruins, many temples, and two national museums.

▶ *Chiang Mai.* The second largest city in Thailand contains ancient temples and street markets offering many kinds of handicrafts.

▶ *Damnoen Saduak Floating Market.* A colorful place to shop for souvenirs, produce, flowers, and other goods sold by vendors from boats on canals.

▶ *Grand Palace, Bangkok.* Large compound in the heart of the city, enclosing temples, public buildings, former royal residences. The most important structure is the Temple of the Emerald Buddha.

▶ *Khao Yai National Park.* The oldest and most visited of Thailand's national parks, containing many kinds of rare wildlife, low mountains, and a rain forest.

▶ *Phuket.* A popular island resort area, nicknamed Pearl of the South.

Industry: Farmland makes up about 45 percent of Thailand's economy. The chief crops are rice, tapioca, and sugarcane. Manufacturing began to be important to Thailand's economy during the 1970s. Important manufactured products include cement, food products, and chemical products. Tourism contributes greatly to the national income. Each year, millions of tourists from around the world visit Thailand.

Currency: 1 Thai bhat (B) = 100 satang; U.S.$1 = 38.65 B

Weights and measures: Metric system (except for the measure of land, which continues to use traditional Thai measures)

Literacy:	88.8%	
Common Thai words and phrases:	Hello, good morning, or good-bye	*Sawatdi krap* (by a male)
		Sawatdi kah (by a female)
	How are you?	*Sabai di ru?*
	I'm fine	*Sabai di*
	Excuse me	*Khothot*
	Thank you	*Khopkhun*
	What is your name?	*Khun chu arai?*
	Foreigner	*Farang*
	Never mind, or It doesn't matter	*Mai pen rai*
	Fun, joyousness	*Sanuk*
Famous People:	King Bhumibol Adulyadej *Rama IX, King of Thailand*	(1927–)
	Chun Likphai *Prime minister*	(1938–)
	Pibol Songgram *Military leader and prime minister*	(1897–1964)

Rama IX

To Find Out More

Nonfiction

▶ Schwabach, Karen. *Thailand, Land of Smiles*. Minneapolis: Dillon Press, Inc., 1991.

▶ Wright, David K., and MaryLee Knowlton. *Children of the World, Thailand*. Milwaukee: Gareth Stevens Publishing, 1988.

Fiction

▶ Ho, Kwoncjan. *Sing to the Dawn*. New York: Lothrop, Lee & Shepard Company, 1975.

▶ Oliviero, Jamie. *Sam See and the Magic Elephant*. New York: Hyperion Books for Children, 1995.

Websites

▶ **Bangkok Post**
http://www.bangkokpost.net
The Internet edition of the English-language Thai newspaper

▶ **Thailand Monarch's Homepage**
http://sunsite.au.ac.th/thailand/rama9/index.html
Information about the king of Thailand, the fiftieth anniversary of his assumption to the throne, and his work as an artist

▶ **Tourism Authority of Thailand**
http://www.tat.or.th/
Food, festivals, events, and province-by-province information

▶ **Royal Thai Embassy**
http://www.thaiembdc.org
Homepage for Thailand's embassy to the United States

Organizations and Embassies

▶ **Royal Thai Embassy**
1024 Wisconsin Avenue, N.W.
Suite 401
Washington, DC 20007
(202) 944-3600
E-mail: thai.wsn@thaiembdc.org

▶ **Tourism Authority of Thailand**
5 World Trade Center
3443
New York, NY 10048
(212) 432-0433

Index

Page numbers in *italics* indicate illustrations.

Khmer Empire, 35
khon (masked drama and dance), 108, *108*
Khon Kaen, 71
Khorat, 71
Khorat Plateau, 15
kickboxing, 110, *110*
kite-flying, 110

L

lacquerware, 104, *104*
language, 36, 77
Lekagul, Boonsong, 20
Lent, 88–89
Likphai, Chun, 133
limestone, 29
literature, 109
Loi Krathong festival, 118–120, *119*

M

Mae Ping River, 75
Mahidol (Rama VIII), 44–45, *45*
mahouts (elephant trainers), 25
mangrove forests, 29
manufacturing, 65, 68, 69
maps
    Bangkok, *51*
    geographical, *16*
    geopolitical, *10*
    historical, *43*
    population, *76*
    primary land use, *19*
    resources, *19*
marine life, 13, 23
    sea turtles, *32–33*
    Tarutao National Park, 32
marriage, 82, *82*
Mekong Delta, *114*
Mekong River, 15, *62*
metal casting, 73
military, 52, *52*
mining, 17, 65, 76
Ministry of Justice, 50

Mo, Khunying. *See* Suranari, Tao.
Mongkut (Rama IV), 40, *40*, *41*, 83
monks, *87*, 88–89, 91, *91*
monsoons, 17
mountains, 14
music, 107, *107*, 126
    national anthem, 51
    royal anthem, 51
Muslim religion, 76, 94, *94*, 95

N

nagas (Hindu deities), 93
names, 78
national anthem, 51
National Assembly, 52
national flag, 50, *50*
National Museum, 98, *98*
national parks, 20–21, *20*
natural resources, 16, 25
nielloware (silverwork), 106

O

orchids, 18, *18*
ordination, 9, 89

P

peafowl, *30*
people, 9, 74, 80, *113*, *125*, 126, *127*.
    See also Famous people.
    chao khao (mountain people),
        79
    children, 112–113, 115
    Chinese descendants, 74–75
    clothing, 121
    education, 43–44, 83, *107*, 115
    farang (foreigner), 9
    Hmong, *74*
    housing, 117, *117*, 124, *125*
    language, 77
    mahouts (elephant trainers), 25
    marriage, 82, *82*
    names, 78

Meet the Author

SYLVIA MCNAIR was born in Korea and believes she inherited a love of travel from her missionary parents. She grew up in Vermont. After graduating from Oberlin College, she held a variety of jobs, married, had four children, and settled in the Chicago area. She now lives in Evanston, Illinois. She is the author of several travel guides and more than a dozen books for young people published by Children's Press.

"Thailand has been one of my favorite countries ever since my first visit more than twenty years ago. I've been back several times, and I learn more about it every time. In between visits, I've been reading as much as I can about the country.

"One of the nicest things about today's technology is that it is so much easier than it used to be to keep in touch with

friends in other countries. I can send a question to the other side of the globe, by fax or e-mail, and have an answer back the same day.

"I love to travel, and I love writing about faraway places. Maybe some of you readers of this book will get an impression of Thailand that inspires you to go and see it for yourselves someday. In the meantime, get a taste of the country by visiting a Thai restaurant. There are hundreds of them in North American cities now."

McNair has traveled in more than forty countries and in all fifty of the United States.

Photo Credits